RENAULT

HECTOR MACKENZIE-WINTLE

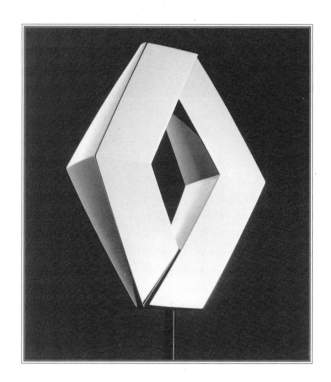

SUTTON PUBLISHING LIMITED

Sutton Publishing Limited
Phoenix Mill · Thrupp · Stroud
Gloucestershire · GL5 2BU

First published 1998

Copyright © Hector Mackenzie-Wintle, 1998

British Library Cataloguing in Publication Data
A catalogue record for this book is available from the
British Library.

ISBN 0-7509-1924-8

Typeset in 10/12 Perpetua.
Typesetting and origination by
Sutton Publishing Limited.
Printed in Great Britain by
Ebenezer Baylis, Worcester.

ACKNOWLEDGEMENTS

Above all, this book is dedicated to Him, without whom we have nothing and through whose mercy I am alive and well today.

It is further dedicated to my best friend and dear wife, Sheila, who has been a constant source of encouragement, a positive critic and a hard-working secretary, to my sons, Andrew and Neil and to my late father, a splendid wordsmith from another generation and in another genre.

For long-term support and access to the company's press photographs and records through the Renarchive Service, I am indebted to Tim Jackson and his Press Office colleagues at Renault UK.

Also I would like to remember John Henderson (for a window of opportunity), Brian Whiteside (for many years of mutual enthusiasm), Tony Parfitt (for invariably sound advice), the late Tony Ronald (for encouraging my interest in the Renault marque from early on), Frank and Clive Stroud and Mike Treacy of Chater & Scott Group (for a companionable business interlude), as well as many Renault and Alpine friends I have made over the years.

Lastly, a sincere thank you to my publisher, Rupert Harding, who has taken the risk of letting me loose with pen and paper. I hope that his faith will have been well founded.

Apart from my own photographs, if I have used any that are not the copyright of the Renault organization, I apologize unreservedly for any unintentional trespass.

Hector Mackenzie-Wintle, Ferndown, 1998

CONTENTS

Louis Renault was born on 12 February 1877, third son of Alfred and Louise Berthe (née Magnien), at their Paris home. He was an indifferent student and an inveterate 'tinkerer', fascinated by things mechanical. Once, he stowed away on a locomotive's coal tender to be sent home in disgrace upon discovery. He was granted a patent and sold the rights to someone else before he converted his three-wheeler de Dion into a four-wheeler *voiturette* (light car). This car pitched him into the motor manufacturing business almost by chance and, with initial orders for a dozen cars, the firm his brothers founded became one of France's industrial engines. The death of his older brother, Marcel, in a 1902 racing car accident and of his eldest brother, Fernand, through ill health left Louis as *patron absolu* (sole owner) by 1909 and he consolidated the company's fortunes through his incredible activity during the First World War, which produced a huge plethora of martial paraphernalia. His single-minded passion for his beloved Billancourt made him France's richest and most powerful industrialist. He was impervious to the bankruptcy of his adversary, Citroën, to the hatred he engendered in many of his workers by his ruthlessness, to the envy of many of his peers and to the suspicion he evoked among politicians. The wartime problems Louis faced were insoluble and, in hindsight, it was easy for his enemies to criticize his decisions; the inevitable results and his declining health made him an ideal scapegoat for their own inadequacies or a target for their revenge.

INTRODUCTION

On 24 December 1898, through the biting Parisian Christmas Eventide wind, a small, four-wheeled, combustion-engined contraption chugged its way smokily uphill to the rue Lépic. It was carrying its constructor, Louis Renault and his brother, Marcel, to dinner in Paris' Montmartre district to celebrate Louis' twenty-first birthday. The vehicle was Louis' hobby, a tiller-steered, homespun *voiturette*, powered by a front-mounted, single-cylinder de Dion engine. Louis spent part of the evening taking his party companions for rides along the neighbouring streets which surrounded *L'Eglise du Sacré Coeur* (the Church of the Sacred Heart). By the small hours, he found himself possessed of twelve enthusiastic buyers' deposits against replicas of his lightweight machine. Perforce and in spite of himself, Louis discovered that his passion for things mechanical had set him on the road to becoming a motor manufacturer.

Louis came from a well-to-do Parisian family who had a house in that city's moneyed rue de Rivoli; their wealth was derived from a drapery business and a button-making factory. Unsurprisingly, they had a country residence in Boulogne-Billancourt (nowadays part of the Parisian urban sprawl) and it was here that Louis, free from the financial necessity of earning a 'proper' living, invented and tinkered with things mechanical. He had rigged up a crude system of electric lighting at home, before household electricity was commonplace; he had already been granted a patent when he was barely twenty and his light car was based on a de Dion tricycle, but noticeably improved. Marcel persuaded his elder brother, Fernand, to bankroll the fledgling undertaking and Louis started manufacturing the first few machines in the garden shed at Billancourt. Thus began the amazing adventure, which was to take the name of Renault all over the world.

Louis was mechanically intuitive and a pragmatist and his cars were simple and lightweight; from the outset, he used direct-drive top gear, shaft transmission and a rear-axle differential at a time when all other makers employed indirect gearing and belts or chains to propel their vehicles. Marcel's and Louis' competition wins in their lightweight cars – often defeating vehicles of much greater engine power – filled the order books to overflowing; beating the Arlsberg Express from Paris to Vienna, where Marcel arrived in the Prater at midday, before the marshals were in place, was astonishing.

Sales targets were annihilated – thirty vehicles were proposed for 1899, yet 179 were sold! Only 4 years later, 600 persons were producing a hundred times that target. Each new model was given an alphabetical letter and such was the pace of progress and diversity that the same year saw the introduction of the Type N. In France, Renault quickly eclipsed the established names and was the country's second largest car manufacturer (behind Peugeot) when the First World War began. Szisz won the first-ever Grand Prix (1906) for Renault; early aviators relied on Renault engines; the famous Renault AG *Taxi de la Marne* was immortalized through troop carrying and the first-ever practical light tank (the Renault FT-17) terrified the German foot soldiers on the Western Front. Splittable spark plugs, direct drive, servo brakes and much else were patented by the ever-inventive Louis, who also founded SEV (Société Anonyme pour l'Equipment Electrique des Vehicules) to break Bosch's stranglehold in the electrical equipment market.

Renault's production range was enormous; the little Type KJs and Type NNs of the 1920s were still trundling around in the '50s; the huge 40CVs smashed world endurance records; Renault-engined Caudron aeroplanes competed against the best in the world and won; the marque triumphed in the Monte Carlo Rally; the famous, six-wheeled passenger vehicles criss-crossed the deserts of Africa and special Renault coaches ran regular scheduled services throughout that region.

Time has blurred Louis' character. He was private and taciturn unless enthused, when his words came tumbling out, but he was ruthless in his pursuit of power, money and women and the development of his factories and his estate at Herqueville. He was ungenerous and a hard task master, considering his workers as a means of producing goods to consolidate his factory. A leader of men he was not, but he was able to motivate others by his enthusiasm, demonstrating practically what had to be done and then expecting it to be done perfectly. He was deeply disappointed that his son, Jean-Louis, was not 'a chip off the old block' – in spades. Louis' sexual powers are alleged to have been considerable and, caring little for society, he was adjudged by many to be uncouth. Yet, while Citroën lit up the Eiffel Tower, dazzled everyone with his famous 'traction' and went bankrupt, Louis (already sole master of his huge empire for decades) eschewed such vulgarity and plodded solidly along, cunningly countering every opponent's advance with a cheaper alternative and ploughing enormous sums of money back into his beloved Ile de Séguin and adjacent Billancourt to make them commercially impregnable. He later paid dearly for all his single-mindedness and autocracy.

Louis admired Hitler's idea of the KdF (Volkswagen), but he was no politician and loved Germans no more than any other race. Renault stood for the Renault party and he could not comprehend losing his empire to the victorious Germans. He faced a no-win choice: refuse to co-operate with the enemy and his factories and remaining staff would be deported to Germany, but co-operate and he would be accused of collaboration. He chose the latter and, despite 'losing' an unbelievable quantity of all kinds of allocated raw materials, the RAF bombed his factories for his pains. Convinced of his innocence, he stayed in France, was unjustly incarcerated and died under very unusual circumstances which have left a number of awkward questions unanswered. As all formal charges against him were dropped in 1951, he was never found guilty, yet his commercial empire was seized completely without financial recompense and was nationalized by de Gaulle to become Régie Nationale des Usines Renault (RNUR).

Nevertheless – and contrary to all expectations – an equally amazing saga then unfolded. Contemporary works make apparent the radically socialist ethos which pervaded and replaced Louis' authoritarianism and, as the Renault marque championed by Pierre Lefaucheux rose phoenix-like from the ashes of war, every new record was hailed enthusiastically. The increasing cadence of 4CV production consolidated the organization, and subsequent model diversification led Renault into new markets. It is clear that Lefaucheux's burning desire to allow the workers' efforts to be fairly rewarded was a cornerstone of this enthralling story.

Over the next five decades, out of thirty or so mainstream models, very few failed to achieve a million sales. Such was the fame of the Dauphine (the only car ever to win the four major European rallies) that many thought it was Renault's first car. The 4CVs ran at Le Mans and were sold through the Sears Roebuck mail order catalogue in the USA. The Frégate broke the world's record for the Cape to Algiers dash (later lowered by a Twelve Gordini) and the 'Shooting Star' gas turbine car set world speed records which still stand at the end of the twentieth century. The go-anywhere Four, launched by leaving dozens around in Paris for the public to test drive, became a legend in its lifetime. The Eight (through the Coupe Gordini) prepared French *pilotes* for the highest ranks of motorsport. Renault-based Alpine won rallies all over the globe and was world rally champion; an Alpine-Renault A-442 won Le Mans outright. Renault pioneered and made a success of turbocharging in Formula One (in the face of the established hierarchy's scepticism) as well as in large-scale passenger vehicle production; the Sixteen was the world's first series-produced true hatchback/liftback and the inimitable Five was the first of the superminis. Renault perceived a winner in Matra's ground-breaking prototype Espace MPV (multi-purpose vehicle) and productionized it, while the cheeky faced Twingo brought humour, space and economy back into inexpensive motoring. Despite top-class opposition, Renault engines, using pneumatic valve technology, completely dominated Formula One for almost a decade and the Laguna was British Touring Car Champion. The Mégane family was exemplary of common-platform technology and the Scénic MAC (multi activity car) pioneered a concept which caught all the competition flat-footed. Renault has been on the podium of COTY (Car of the Year) winners often and the company's concept cars – Mégane, Laguna, Scénic, Ludo, Initiale, Racoon, Pangea and Zo, to name but a few – have made the organization synonymous with innovative ideas.

Without considering any of the social benefits pioneered by Renault, the full list of post-war achievements is no less astonishing than that which Louis established during his reign. But even more surprising is the fact that a succession of gifted leaders – Lefaucheux, Dreyfus, Vernier-Palliez, Hanon, Besse, Lévy and Schweitzer – were able to perform these feats with a nationalized organization. For much of its life, the organization has been hindered by its rules of foundation from either competing on equal terms with the world's most powerful international private enterprise vehicle producers or from receiving any no-strings financial state aid, so that organic growth was virtually self-financed from retained profits. It was forced to raise money either through redeemable public bonds or via interest-loaded government loans, yet was unable to reap the advantages of company share dealing. Nevertheless, despite the cyclic nature of the industry in general, the RNUR has been profitable over the years, as its growth testifies. As financing has changed in the 1990s, so the status of the organization has been modified to allow individual share ownership, thus transforming its earlier structure and ensuring a more competitive position for the future.

In so concise a book it is difficult to do adequate justice to this truly international marque, but the following images will illustrate an outstanding patrimony and confirm the vibrant presence of a creative organization, which is fully determined to stride triumphantly towards its bicentenary.

CHAPTER ONE

THE EARLY YEARS

Louis Renault's first workshop. It looks like a garden shed with a barbecue, but this was the Renault family's rural villa's shed, complete with forge, in which Louis converted his single-cylinder de Dion tricycle into his own first prise directe *(direct drive) Type A in 1898. From these humble beginnings grew his beloved Billancourt. It still stands (regrettably in somewhat modernized form) in a garden, overlooked now by the Renault HQ office, but factories and cities do not mix and manufacturing has been transferred elsewhere. Shortly, the site will be razed to the ground for new development.*

INTRODUCTION

Ever since the start of the Industrial Revolution there have been areas of rapid advance, followed by consolidation: steam power, canals, shipbuilding, railways, cars, aeroplanes, computers. Brunel, Stephenson, Ford, Gates and others were remarkable men of vision or application (or both) in their time. Louis Renault was one such, probably the greatest in France overall in his field; a pioneer, a creator, a pragmatist, a calculator and persistent – perhaps obstinate – to the end. Born in 1877, Louis was the youngest of five children whose father, Alfred, was a self-made bourgeois draper with a button factory. He despaired of Louis, an inveterate *bricoleur* (tinkerer), but that pastime set him on the road to becoming one of Europe's leading vehicle manufacturers within fifteen years.

His first car was not a hit-or-miss affair, like many of the self-propelled vehicles being constructed at the time. It was based on a proven design, the de Dion tricycle, cleverly modified into a four-wheeler with the drive transmitted first through a three-speed gearbox, in which top was a direct drive, then via a transmission shaft, which finally converted the engine power through 90° to turn the rear wheels. Lightness, flexibility and quietness characterized the design at a time when power-sapping, clattering chains and squealing belts were the norm in car transmissions.

Renault Frères was founded by Louis' elder brothers to exploit patent no. 285,753 (09/02/99) 'Direct Drive' as well as others to help to finance the manufacture of the first cars. Marcel was in charge, Fernand controlled the finances, Louis organized the manufacturing and, within six months, sixty cars had been sold, including probably the world's first closed model, bodied by Labourdette.

The brothers Renault realized early on that their light, manoeuvrable and (comparatively) reliable vehicles could compete with – and often beat – the contemporary monsters. Unable to afford professional drivers, they drove their cars themselves. On 28 August 1899, a Renault won the Paris–Trouville race in just over four and a half hours; three days later, they came first and second in the Paris–Ostend event and the following month, Louis beat Marcel to the post, averaging over 36kph for the Paris–Rambouillet race. The marque's fame spread quickly and, at the 1900 Universal Exhibition, they exhibited 'series manufactured' models, which became increasingly popular with every new victory, such as their one-two-three-four class win in the 552 km-long Paris–Bordeaux race. Marcel triumphed over the only other class finishers in the light car category – all Renaults – in the gruelling 1,137 km Paris–Toulouse–Paris race, which produced 350 orders.

Cars began to outgrow their obvious horse-drawn carriage ancestry and the lighter ones used spoked wheels rather than heavy wooden artillery wheels. Louis quickly discarded tiller steering in favour of a steering wheel and a backwards-raked steering column. Other adoptions included (at least partially) enclosed coachwork and water-cooling instead of air-cooling for the increasingly powerful engines, this being effected initially by gilled radiator tubes along either side of the engine cover. From 1904, the radiator was mounted behind the engine, protruding each side past the line of the waterfall engine cover, a silhouette which was to become a Renault hallmark up to the end of the 1920s.

Renault's entire competition focus was changed by the tragic death of Marcel in the ill-fated 1903 Paris–Madrid race. Blinded by dust, he had entered a left-hand bend at Bourg-de-Vay, near Couhé-Vérac, too fast and the car slid off the road and somersaulted, and he was dashed into a fatal coma. Race-leader by Bordeaux, Louis retired all the Renaults upon learning of his brother's injuries and he never again drove in any competition. Distraught, he thought to give up the whole business, but, upon learning that Marcel had left his share of the company to his girlfriend, Suzanne Davenay, 'une danseuse, petite, blonde insignifiante' – 'a little, insignificant, blonde dancer' (Saint Loup), he persuaded her to sell him her shares 'in this precarious motor car business' for an annual income and a new Renault car every year. This deal was faithfully honoured – even after Louis' death – by la Régie until her own death, long after the end of the Second World War.

At the same time, Fernand showed his mettle; he sold his shares in the button-making business and became fully involved in the factory. Louis started inventing again – a splittable spark plug, an hydraulic damper, a compressed air starter, operable from the driver's seat, to name but a few products. In 1907, he designed and produced his first aero engine (an air-cooled V8).

The little twin-cylinder Type AG, with its new-fangled taximeter, began to make inroads into the taxi-cab market, the first Renault buses appeared on the Parisian streets, as did road sprayer/sweepers, and Renault lorries started to haul freight along the routes nationales. A win for the marque in the (first ever) 1906 Grand Prix de l'ACF (Automobile Club de France), thanks largely to the pioneering detachable-rim Michelin wheels which minimized puncture downtime, allied with strategic driving by Ferenc Szisz, set the firm on a path of explosive growth, both at home and overseas.

In 1908, Fernand became ill and was forced to retire, so Louis bought his shares. He was now truly master of Billancourt and a man of whom it was written, 'the daring of his ideas, his independence of spirit, his appreciation of his times . . . his prodigious capacity for work, made him the most complete captain of industry in the first half of the century' (Lucien Dauvergne). In fact, he had been made a Chevalier de la Légion d'honneur in 1906 in deference to his services to the automobile industry and to his country.

By the end of the decade, the firm was employing over 10,000 workers and business was booming. But the palmy days were coming to an end.

This is the very car which started the Renault adventure in 1898. It is a hotch-potch of bicycle technology (wire-wheels with bolts and wing nuts holding the beaded-edge tube/tyre onto the rim), motorcycle/tricycle engineering (air-cooled engine and contracting brakes), horse-drawn carriage ancestry (oil lamps, bodywork and seating arrangements) and railway construction (leaf springs and lever controls), all topped off with semi-circular tiller steering (very soon to be discarded in favour of a circular steering wheel), transmission brake and a direct top gear, driving the back axle via a solid propeller shaft.

Marcel Renault is seated in the front seat of a de Dion with Louis in the centre, his car with the 'meatsafe' engine cover removed, revealing the reality of his lightweight machine. Paul Hugé, an early collaborator, at right, steers an 1899 'pukka' production Type A, with the engine cover in situ and the bulb horn on the tiller. Note that the vertical tiller handles on Louis' car are absent, suggesting this may be a 1900 photograph with the prototype car still being used for developments, such as a round steering wheel – see the position of Louis' right hand.

Renault Type B, 1900. Renault's final air-cooled engine — still a de Dion of 450cc capacity — powered this, possibly the first ever, enclosed car, looking much like a sedan chair without carrying poles plonked on to bicycle wheels. The construction, by Labourdette, provided a flat windscreen to protect the ensconced travellers, an exhaust silencer (for the first time) to quieten things down and double elliptic springs to smooth the (shock-absorberless) ride.

Renault Type C, 1900. At the turn of the century, this was a sophisticated little town runabout. The Type B saloon of Labourdette seen earlier has here a worthy successor and perhaps the *carrossier* (coachbuilder) was the same, although now there is a little outside seat at the back – for the chauffeur perhaps, the dog, the mother-in-law or the postillion? Although invisible here, the steering column topped by a wheel was almost certainly vertical and the 'meat safe' engine cover has been replaced by one carrying the single-cylinder de Dion engine's coolant through the gilled tubes on either side.

Renault Type C, 1901. Louis Renault sits at the wheel of his single-cylinder, 8hp de Dion (100 x 130 mm) engined racer before the 1901 Paris–Bordeaux race, in which he finished twelfth overall and first in the *voiturette* (light car) class, followed by Marcel Renault, Oury and Grus in similar cars. Only half the competitors even finished, the winner being Fournier on a 60hp Mors, so the performance of the Renaults was outstanding.

Renault Type D, 1901. Because of the artisanal nature of early car manufacturing, changes were constant, so the identification of this model is made on the basis of the one-piece mudguard-cum-running board, which, hitherto, had been separate mudguards without running boards, and of the inclined steering column with a steering wheel. Power for this 6CV was still provided by either Aster or de Dion single-cylinder, water-cooled engines, with lateral gilled radiators. The three-speed gearbox used Louis' *prise directe* and, unusually, this car is running on wooden-spoked, not wire-spoked, road wheels.

'The Top Brass', 1902. Every inch the dapper businessmen of their day, Marcel Renault (left), Louis Renault (centre) and Paul Hugé, works manager, pose in front of a new piece of machinery waiting to be installed to earn its keep in the Billancourt works. It is difficult to discern the tousle-haired, usually oil-covered *bricoleur* (tinkerer) who was Louis beneath the *melon* (bowler hat) and stood on polished shoes or to believe that, within six years, Marcel would have been killed, Fernand would have died and Louis would own the entire business.

Renault Type NC, 1903. This two-cylinder 10CV 'thumper' with a three-speed gearbox is typical of the small Renaults of the period. There are artillery wheels, no front brakes and the coachbuilt body is by Kellner et ses Fils. The 'C303' may indicate that this is the 303rd vehicle bodied by this firm and the gilled radiator enables accurate dating. The passenger(s) swung the front 'windscreen' open, then pushed the two lower doors forward from the middle and made the appropriately graceful exit. The whole ensemble still recalls vehicles of a horse-drawn age.

Renault Frères Factory, 1903. This is the main gate of 'Renault Frères: Ateliers et Bureaux' (works and offices), established within five years of the first prototype chugging out of Louis' shed. By this time, the work force had grown from 500 in 1902 to 600, producing 9 different Renault models, totalling 1,600 vehicles per annum, nearly three times the previous year's output, and the factory area had almost quadrupled in size over this same period. To judge by the shadows, it is probably early morning in this still-rural Parisian suburb, but there does not seem to be too much activity.

Renault Type O-B Vanderbilt Cup Racer, 1904. After Marcel Renault's 1902 Paris–Madrid Race death, the factory withdrew from racing. This four-cylinder, 12.3-litre 60/90CV unique car was built for the rich American, Gould Brookaw, who had Maurice Bernin drive it in this famous race on 8 October 1907, where a driveshaft broke after the first lap. Six weeks later, it claimed the course record at the Eagle Rock, New York venue. The car had a tubular chassis, a streamlined bonnet and a huge, fan-cooled, circular gilled radiator behind the engine.

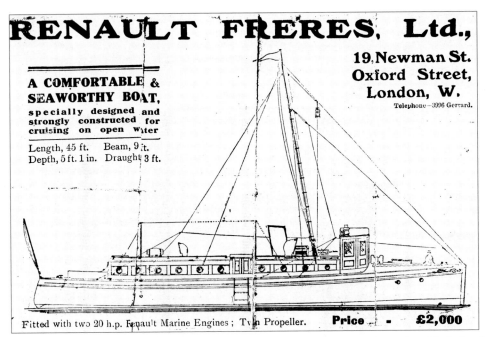

Renault Motor Cruiser, 1904. Louis Renault was enthused by anything mechanical and had already obtained patents and built a motor boat, *The Gigolo*, long before he built cars. He nearly drowned in it, too, because the freeboard was too low, but he escaped, learned quickly and the steam-powered *Gigolo II* received its Certificate of Sea Worthiness in due course. This advertisement does not tell us whether or not it was a Renault boat or if it merely used two Renault marine engines. But, according to the dimensions, it was no little dinghy and £2,000 was a lot of money in those days.

Renault Type AG Coupé, 1905. Once again, this vehicle is reminiscent of a horse-drawn carriage, with the chauffeur at the mercy of the elements and with lights certainly designed to be seen by rather than to see with. The Type AG, whose pinnacle of fame was attained later as the unforgettable *Taxi de la Marne*, was the taxi equivalent of the later Type AX, an indestructible two-cylinder, four-stroke lugger which survived untold maltreatment. It developed 8bhp at a heady 1500rpm and the three-speed gearbox used Louis' patented *prise directe*. The flyaway mudguards add a certain jauntiness to the whole ensemble.

Renault 14/20 Landaulette, 1906. King Edward VII purchased this Hooper-bodied vehicle, the first time a Renault had resided in the Royal Mews. The thermo-syphon cooling radiator was still just in front of the windscreen and behind the engine, which was enclosed by the Renault hallmark coalscuttle bonnet. The engine was pressure-lubricated and an exhaust gas pressure-driven pump supplied the fuel. The unusually fine engine pick-up and elegant luxury appealed to the sybaritic monarch and the vehicle remained in the royal fleet well into King George V's reign.

Renault's Billancourt works, 1906. It is interesting to compare this view with that on p. 16; in three years the factory size doubled and, although the building on the right has remained virtually unchanged, the country house to the left has been demolished and replaced with a not displeasing factory building. The gateway is wider with very substantial portals, the side gate has moved from right to left and there is a more impressive sign. By 1906, the number of workers had risen from 600 to 1,500 and vehicle production had jumped from 1,600 to over 2,200.

Renault Type AR Triple Phaeton, 1908. This model was a main attraction on Renault's November 1907 Paris Salon stand; the 54bhp (at 1200rpm), 9.5-litre engine was Billancourt's first six-cylinder unit (in three blocks of two cylinders) and it was coupled to a four-speed gearbox, on the highest ratio of which a speed of over 70mph could be attained. Another patented feature was a compressed air starter, which could also be used to inflate the tyres. Make no mistake, this was a formidable machine in its day and, with this skimpy coachwork, it was no slouch.

Renault Type AT Racer, 1909. Louis Raffalovich, who had got to know Louis Renault when they were educated together for a while, was in America and was engaged by Renault Frères' selling branch to drive the car seen here, co-piloted by Basle, in the 24 Hour New York Race at Coney Island in 1909. By having special goggles made and by the astuteness of stopping at the end of the first lap to fit the huge front mudguards seen here, the Renault won the race by a huge margin — three hours and 170 km ahead of the runner up, Rainier. The return to New York, along flower-strewn streets to huge applause, was triumphal.

Renault Type AX, 1909. Here is yet another variation of Louis Renault's *deux pattes* (twin cylinder), this time a 10CV, two-seater saloon with a rear spider seat, which recalls coaching days. This photograph allows us to see the half elliptic springing and the two right-hand levers (handbrake and gear lever), which characterized all Renaults for years. Other interesting features include the relative smallness of the saloon, the bulb of the horn near to the raked steering wheel rim (observe how the serpentine tube emerges), the opening windscreen, the huge lights and the suicide doors.

Renault Type BZ, 1909. Even after ten years, Renaults were still influenced by coaching days – lamps, door handles, rear mudguards, wheels and scant protection for the 'coachman', whose feet were kept warm in cold weather by the adjacent radiator. The gear lever remained to the driver's right, together with a brake operating on the rear drums only; the right-hand foot pedal operated a brake on a drum on the transmission shaft. The long road springs offered plenty of deflection, but there were no shock absorbers to control the rebound. It was very hard to distinguish between the Type BX 14CV, the Type BZ 12CV and the Type BK 10CV.

Renault Type X-1 Double Phaeton, 1909. This was the last of the Type Xs, first seen in 1907. The engine speed (1200rpm) was governed by a speed limiter, and drive through the usual cone clutch to a four-speed gearbox allowed a top speed of around 30mph. This 14CV 3-litre was robust enough to be fitted with a six-seater omnibus body, but the chief interest of the coachwork seen here is the unusual cockpit cowling and the passengers' windscreen, stayed into position by straps, to the top rail of which the rear hood fastened.

Renault AG-1 London taxicab, 1909. Interestingly, the French version appears never to have had a roof for the cabby, whereas the London Cab Company's vehicles appear mostly as seen here. Let us remember that this was an 8CV, two-cylinder, 1205cc, three-speed gearbox vehicle and that, in the event of a puncture, the spare wheel and its special rim (sometimes known as a 'Stepney'), upon which 'George' is resting his elbow, were bolted to the outside of the wounded wheel so that the taxi could reach its garage for a proper exchange repair to be effected, since (whole) detachable wheels were not yet widely available.

CHAPTER TWO

IN THE SHADOW OF THE FIRST WORLD WAR

Renault Type FT-17 Light Tank (char léger) in Paris for the Victory Parade, 1919. Renault produced the first examples in 1917 and personally undertook some of the early testing in the war-torn French countryside. Despite bureaucratic buckpassing, bungling and delays, the vehicle was eventually manufactured at Billancourt and under licence in other French factories (for example, Berliet, SOMUA and Delaunay-Belleville), playing an important role in breaking the First World War deadlock. Built abroad – even in the USA – under licence, it was still in use over twenty years later at the outbreak of the next hostilities.

INTRODUCTION

It is said that war is a mighty accelerator of progress; this is true not only of technological advance, but also of human perception. While the First World War saw little change in the methods of warfare, the means of warfare developed significantly – new weaponry, the introduction of tanks, submarines and aeroplanes, the mechanization of troop and *matériel* movements, naval developments and increased newspaper coverage of the horrors of war. A firm of Renault's size could not remain aloof from these happenings.

In 1910 the Renault factories were flooded, but nothing curbed the marque's expansion. By 1913 over 40,000 units had been sold through the world's most widespread sales network – in Spain, Hungary, Russia, India, New Zealand, Japan, Argentina, USA, England, everywhere. Renault was running neck-and-neck with Ford at Dagenham, but Henry's Model T laid the foundations for the motorization of a whole new class of people on a massive scale and the clouds of war were looming over Europe.

Renault is remembered historically for the *Taxis de la Marne* episode. The Germans had moved towards Paris with lightning speed and, by September 1914, were threatening a demoralized capital. General Galliéni, recently promoted to the military governorship of that city, promised to defend it to the end. With a 600-strong fleet of Renault taxis, 12,000 soldiers were moved within hours to the battlefront where they surprise-attacked the German flank in the early morning, inflicting heavy damage and causing an expensive enemy withdrawal. A pitched five-day battle ensued, which involved 2 million combatants, but it freed Paris and heralded a winter of trench stalemate. The first-ever mechanized mass troop movement thus passed into the history of warfare.

For the war effort Renault produced lorries, machine-guns, heavy artillery and shells and improved aero engine performance, first to 100bhp and then to 130; the propeller was fitted to the half-crankshaft-speed-rotating camshaft and engine cooling was improved by force-feeding air over the finned cylinder barrels. In 1916, Renault built a twelve-cylinder aero engine with aluminium pistons which, producing 300bhp, was fitted to the Bréguet 14s of Vuillemin's famous 12th Squadron, which continuously strafed the retreating German troops.

Renault was the only car manufacturer to produce a workable light tank, the FT-17, which, despite typically bureaucratic wrangling, undertook its first trials early in 1917. Further trials and modifications followed and it eventually saw action at the end of May 1918. By July, over a thousand had been delivered and examples were still being used in the Second World War.

The upheaval of the First World War had far-reaching consequences: France had lost over a million of her young men, those who should have both contributed their working life to their country's able-bodied workforce and been consumers of goods. Louis had been decorated an *Officier de la Légion d'honneur* (the only non-combatant to be thus rewarded) and, like others, his factories had boomed – but now what was to be done? Louis saw the answer – produce more at a lower price. By now the factory area was huge and the means of production quite breathtaking, but the cost of raw materials was yet in the hands of others. Baron Petiet took over the Hagondange steelworks, seized from Germany as war reparations, and Louis founded another company nearby to refine the raw steel into special steels for his vehicles – excellent vertical integration. He continued to produce a large range of vehicles in small(ish) quantities to cover the majority of the market potential.

No picture of the inter-war French automobile industry would be complete without taking into account the fierce struggle between the flamboyant André Citroën and the ruthless Louis Renault. It had taken the 'King of Billancourt' twenty-five years to build up a solid and faultless empire; he never borrowed a sou from the banks, he paid all his suppliers at an average of 3 per cent discount for cash and whenever he issued new shares in the company he personally underwrote the vast majority thereof. He cultivated his factories as a peasant cultivates his land and fortified his domain against every financial crisis.

André Citroën was a spontaneous businessman of the new school: he was no financier – banks were there to see to that sort of thing. He had worked for other motor manufacturers and during the First World War his engineering enterprise had made a considerable amount of money out of manufacturing shells. He aimed to series-produce a single model and the four-seater, 10CV Citroën *torpédo* of 1919 was his first blockbuster. It was reasonably affordable, yet it had everything at the outset – standard bodywork, spare wheel, electric starter and electric lighting – just like Ford in the USA. But it was revolutionary in Europe.

Post-war Renaults looked very like the pre-war family of cars – the same general outline, the hallmark of a coal-scuttle bonnet and the radiator behind the engine. The lack of ready money depressed the sale of cars and innovation from Renault was not forthcoming until the end of the decade – the first left-hand drive cars and engines, with the four cylinders *en bloc*, new springing and factory bodies in response to Citroën's offerings. But the cars still had no brakes on the front axle and still had magneto ignition. They were good, solid, tried and tested goods, yet still profitable, for Louis was not about to pauperize himself.

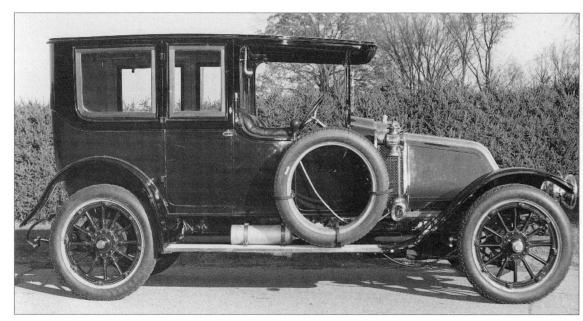

Renault Type AI Phaeton, 1910. This 35CV was introduced in June 1906, one of the first Renaults to use a pressed steel chassis, and it had a 7.5-litre engine and four-speed gearbox driving the artillery type road wheels. Its chassis strength and engine power enabled a wide selection of coachwork to be carried, especially of the limousine and phaeton type, the example seen here being one of the last made and owned in the 1960s by an American living in Ohio. An interesting feature is the communication trumpet strategically placed by the chauffeur's right ear.

Renault Type BY Berline de Voyage, 1910. A new model homologated on 29 December 1909, the Type BY superseded the Type V-1, which had been in production since 1906 and, although the engine and chassis were carried over, the available coachwork area had been increased. The engine was a four-cylinder, 4.3-litre 20CV, coupled to a four-speed gearbox and there were three chassis choices – long, extra long and lightweight. The coachwork on this example was very similar to that on Louis Renault's own car at the time, although his was a Type BM 25CV, four-cylinder car.

Renault Type BK Limousine, 1910. This year's model was unchanged from the 1909 offering, which, in turn, was developed from the Type AM 10CV, originally of 1906. Previously, Renault's four-cylinder engines had been made in two pairs of twin cylinders and Louis had been experimenting with monoblocs since 1905; the Type BK was the first to use it, in 1.7-litre 10CV form. Note the comparative verticality of this car's steering column, which could be raked backwards as an option, the curious 'tween doors mudguard and the upper half of the windscreen folded into the underside of the roof.

Renault AX Voiturette, 1911. This twin-cylinder Renault was manufactured between 1909 and 1913 and this particular one belongs to Renault UK Ltd. The engine was a 1200cc, two-cylinder 'chugger' producing 8bhp at 1500rpm; it had a cone clutch and three-speed gearbox, half-elliptic springs all round and was Renault's first mass-produced car, introduced at the 1908 Paris Salon. It could be supplied with a number of alternative crown wheel and pinion ratios and, over the years, was clothed in a wide variety of coachwork. It was a truly indestructible little classic.

21 Pall Mall, London SW1, 1911. By this time Renault Ltd's status required a prestigious headquarters and showroom in London and so the company bought 'Ye Bell Inn' off St James' Square for £21,000, demolished it and built a bit of Paris in London. Modelled on their Parisian Champs-Elysées showroom (now Pub Renault), complete with French 'Marianne effigies', symbolic of the French Republic, over the windows, Renault had it built with Italian marble floors and mirrored walls and the boardroom was furnished in Louis XIV style. Incidentally, some Renault staff and Renault Owners' Club guests watched the passage of Queen Elizabeth II's 1953 coronation *cortège* from this vantage point, but the building was sold in 1959.

Renault Type CC Double Phaeton, 1912. To distinguish between the different Type C variations on external appearance is very difficult, but the shortness of the bonnet inclines one to a medium-sized vehicle, in this case, a 3.5-litre, four-cylinder, 14CV with Kellner (owing to the front mudguard shape) as the possible coachbuilder. The car was manufactured for Jean Renault, a cousin of Louis, but why does an English AA badge top the radiator header tank? Had it been garnered as part of a European tour or is this just one-upmanship? In any case, the chauffeur will surely be hoping for fine weather!

Renault Type CI Double Phaeton, 1912. The slow-revving, 8.5-litre, 35CV engine produced tremendous torque, which was delivered to the four-speed gearbox via the usual cone clutch. Laclaverie Gache's coachwork offered very stylized mudguards and, while the enormous headlamps and twin — be it noted — audible warning devices were impressive, the most unusual feature is the 'cape cart' hood with discreet rear windows, all of which did nothing for the car's aerodynamics and M. Le Chauffeur was, as ever, out in the cold in this apparently wintry scene. The side lamps show direct descent from the horse-drawn carriage era.

Renault Type AG-1 Fiacre, 1913. Through the years from 1905 one can observe small changes in the perfecting of this vehicle with many developments resulting from feedback from owners and users in cities all over the world. Most of them were produced as a *landaulète décapotable* (convertible coupé), as seen here, and supplied with the Renault-invented taximeters. One Paris company ordered more than 3,000 and there were over 1,000 in London, always with the twin-cylinder 1205cc engine. The Type AG ceased production in 1914.

Renault Type DG Landaulet, 1913. A development of the 1912 Type CB, this model was in production for only the two years before the advent of the First World War. Nominally a 12CV, its 2.6-litre engine produced its maximum power at 1200rpm; there was also a lowered chassis version. The driver, with a cigarillo clamped in his mouth and sporting a *melon*, driving gloves and gaiters over polished shoes, has an air of supreme confidence in his own and his vehicle's capabilities, although the optimistic adjustment of the front lights would not impress an MOT inspector today. The line of the mudguards suggests Kellner as the coachbuilder.

Renault Type AL London Taxi, 1914. Commencing in 1905 with an order from the French Cab Company for 250 taxis, Renault started the mass production of the little *deux pattes* (two-cylinder models), which remained in production, almost unchanged, until 1920 and operated in many capital cities, including Paris, New York and London. Cabby John Stanton poses with his mount, which sports acetylene lamps (with a spare clipped to the running board), pendant communication trumpet and rudimentary two-piece metal weather shield. No wonder he wore a heavy overcoat!

Renault Type ED Coupé Limousine, 1914. The 4.5-litre, four-cylinder engine produced its power at 1440rpm and drove through a cone clutch to the four-speed gearbox. As usual, the rear-wheel (only) brakes were operated by the right-hand lever and the footbrake operated on a drum on the transmission shaft. Electric lighting was an extra, provided by an engine-driven SEV dynamo, but shades of the horse-drawn carriage still linger. Labourdette clothed this particular 18CV, complete with hand-applied wickerwork and it was one of the last civilian models Renault produced before the First World War.

Renault 4WD Tractor, 1914. From 2 to 24 March 1914, the French Minister of War set out an 860-km trial course for military vehicles in eastern France over very varied terrain. This four-cylinder, petrol-fuelled Renault, an army version of the Type GT 40CV, with double, solid rubber-rimmed wheels all round, disengageable front-wheel drive and roll-up front screen and side screens must have been an uncomfortable, noisy, agricultural boneshaker, but it won the competition with its sister car right behind. Afterwards, the vehicles had to be completely dismantled for a thorough inspection by the War Office.

Renault Type EI Cloverleaf Torpédo, 1914. This is the Renault that the 'man-about-town' was driving on the eve of the First World War. It offered a capacity of 4½ litres, shared between four cylinders, pumping out a heady 20hp and driving through a four-speed gearbox; the huge headlights, shiny brass klaxon horn on the running board, an individual step-plate to the dickey seat and fly-away rear mudguards as well as side lights unusually faired into the scuttle of the fashionable coachwork denote the work of the renowned Labourdette.

Renault Experimental Car, 1914. The build year of the vehicle seen here can only be guessed at, based on the general body configuration, the shape of the front bulkhead, the door and handles and the appearance of the wire-wheels. What is known is that it is an early 'special' utilizing an eight-cylinder, 70CV Renault aero engine with geared rear propeller, prepared for winter manoeuvres by Ferdinand de Lesseps, he of Suez Canal fame. The quick-release wheels could be removed for the propeller to blow the contraption over snow-covered surfaces, when it was possibly somewhat effective.

Renault Type DT Torpédo Sport, 1914. During 1913, the Type DT replaced the Type CG, but it was only in production for one year. A 7.5-litre 40CV monster with a four-speed gearbox, it was very similar to the Type CG in specification and price. The machine seen here is clearly stripped to do the business – Weymann fabric bodywork (no headlights, no mudguards, no screen) and the driver has a Teutonic severity about him. The normal vehicle weighed about 2,300 kg and, on the highest final drive ratio, had a top speed of about 55mph.

The Renault depot, Seagrave Road, 1916. This is the earliest photograph known to exist of the Seagrave Road depot in London's Fulham area; regrettably, it is not very sharp. The factory does not appear to be too new, so it was probably not purpose-built by Renault. The war work seems to centre on aero engines, because the V-formation of such machinery can be determined hanging between two wooden trestles on the right, detached from the 'cocks combs' in the background (right), which can be seen on Renault-engined First World War aeroplanes.

Renault FT-17 Tank, 1917. Louis Renault's logical choice to build a light tank was so that it could be transported to the battlefield (or recovered therefrom for repair) on a lorry, which could travel faster to the point of need. Observe how flat-plane plates are bolted together to accelerate repair and reduce expensive first costs. The huge side-boom, rear driving sprocket, front idler and dependent bogey wheels at bottom seem somewhat rudimentary nowadays, but were very effective. Additionally, the FT's turret was manoeuvrable through 360°, which was revolutionary, and the skid plate at the back ensured that the machine could not topple over backwards.

Bréguet 14, 1918. Although Renault started to build aero engines in the early days of the twentieth century, it became a major manufacturer of these power plants during the First World War. Bréguet was a well-known aeroplane manufacturer and, having used a number of proprietary engines previously, accepted Renault as one of their major engine suppliers. This is a plane from the famous Vuillemin Squadron, a scourge of the enemy lines, and one can see the major advances in streamlining and aeronautics, which martial necessity had demanded in a few short years.

Renault Voiture de Livraison, 1918. Although small delivery vans for the Paris area before the First World War were often twin-cylinder machines, vans for heavier loads were likely to be of the 16CV, four-cylinder variety. This photograph is believed have been taken in the 1920s and, although the vans have early (flat top) bonnets and radiators (square corners), they have balloon tyres and eight-stud plate wheels, doubled at the back to take the extra loads, which suggest modification in the 1920s. The coachwork is à la mode and there are full windscreens. Perhaps these are refurbished and updated war-time lorries because the front mudguards look modern too?

Renault Type GR Torpédo, 1919. This was a lightweight version of the Type PS 18CV, homologated on 12 September 1919 and having the same wheelbase as the 12CV Type EU, but being shorter overall. The monobloc, four-cylinder, 4.5-litre engine gave a top speed of over 50mph to this factory bodied model, which cost 20,000F at the time, and it was black leather-trimmed, with carpets throughout. Single-frame hood, sidescreens, sidelights, bulb horn or klaxon, spare wheel frame with spare rim and rear luggage rack were among the many extras offered.

Renault Type GS Berline, 1919. The first post-war Paris Salon took place in October 1919 and Renault commercialized this model (homologated on 30 October 1919) with a monobloc, four-cylinder, 2.1-litre engine in direct response to Citroën's 10CV launch. Buyers were faced with a choice: a new and attractive car from a new and unknown manufacturer or a greatly improved one from a known manufacturer of twenty years' standing? Note a knobbly tyre and a smooth one mounted diagonally opposite a similar one, a common practice of the period, and left-hand-drive for the first time.

CHAPTER THREE

THE 'ROARING TWENTIES'

*Renault Type NM Record Breaker, 1926. Whereas the 1925 record-breaking Renault had been based on the
Type MC standard chassis, with a Lavocat et Marsaud Grand Sport torpedo body devoid of its mudguards,
the succeeding machine was based on a later chassis with a special lightweight, narrow, wind-cheating body,
built on the Weymann principle, namely leathercloth stretched over wooden formers. Centre-lock 'Rudge'
wire-wheels replaced the heavier artillery type wheels and the front bulkhead was lowered by sloping the
radiator backwards. The drivers, Plessier, Garfield and Guillon are seen here with the flower-bedecked,
victorious monster.*

INTRODUCTION

Because there was little money around after the First World War, one had to sell at whatever cost in order to survive. Citroën's glitzy entry into the car market forced the solid Louis to respond: in 1922, he introduced the production line to Billancourt and revolutionized his manufacturing capacity. Output rose from 10,700 in 1920 to 53,000 in 1930, peaking at 59,700 in 1927.

The two-cylinder cars had been phased out at the end of the previous decade and an extensive range of four-cylinder cars now formed the mainstay of Renault's business, while the six-cylinder cars, with up to some 9 litres' engine capacity, continued to top the range. In 1921, Renault responded to Citroën with the little monobloc, 951cc Type KJ 6CV, which had a detachable cylinder head and three-speed gearbox.

The following year saw the first major external change to the Renault frontal appearance since before the First World War: the radiator became enclosed in a new, louvred front bulkhead and the engine was covered with a modernized alligator-type bonnet, on the front of which was mounted a new, round Renault badge. At the top end of the range, the famous 40CV engine and chassis (used by French presidents, but still with archaic wooden wheels) rode serenely onwards to be clothed by the best coachmakers – Million-Guiet, Vanden Plas, Letourneur, Kellner, Boulogne, Driguet, Galle and many others – although the modernized six-cylinder engine was now a monobloc and front wheel brakes were fitted.

Besides this, Renault was producing tracked tractors, light motorized rail locomotives, aero engines and twelve-wheeler exploration vehicles (twin wheels on each end of the three axles, the back two of which were driven, with two spares at the back), as a riposte to Citroën's Kégresse half-tracks. Also, Renault started to manufacture diesel engines and in 1927 the French Navy adopted these; by 1929, Renault was offering heavy commercial vehicles powered in the same way. And patent applications were lodged by the dozen. But the value of publicity to increase sales became a powerful spur, encouraged by the opening of the Montlhéry track in 1924.

In real estate terms, this decade saw Louis turn the enterprise into a limited company (separate from his own immense fortune) and consolidate his empire. The Ile de Séguin became one huge island factory, tethered to Billancourt by a single iron bridge. Renault's factories covered 100 hectares, an area larger than the city of Chartres, and 30,000 people worked for this manufacturer. The undertaking was immense for the period.

There was a tremendous interest in record breaking on land, sea and air. In 1924, the little Type KJ grew up into the Type NN (now with front brakes) and two years later an example covered 16,000 km at the Miramas track (now abandoned) in 203 hours, including 3 hours of pit stops (one for a violent storm and two to repair the vehicle following a fire during refuelling). This was a real money-spinner for Louis and its unburstability became proverbial; over 200,000 were sold by 1927.

The famous 10CV six-wheelers, with a front-mounted winch to pull themselves out of difficulty, could cover 900 km without refuelling and in 1923 three of them linked the Algerian railhead at Colomb-Béchar to its counterpart in Niger, thus establishing the feasibility of a regular, commercial, wheeled-vehicle, trans-Sahara link. One vehicle pushed on non-stop to Bouréma (Niger) to cover a total trans-desert journey of 2,400 km and, having explored the Upper Niger, completed the return journey to Algiers to triumphal acclaim. Shortly afterwards, Renault Type OXs began a regular trans-Sahara service. Even more amazing, Commander Delinguette and his wife left Colomb-Béchar in their 10 CV Renault on 15 November 1925 and arrived in Capetown on 3 July 1926 after an heroic trans-continental solo journey. Others, all Renault-mounted, drove from Egypt to Karachi via Palestine, Lebanon, Mesopotamia, Persia and Baluchistan. (Readers may need an atlas to identify these place, mostly now renamed.) These exploits are but a few examples of many successfully undertaken by Renault vehicles.

But perhaps the most publicity was gained by Renault's record attempts at Montlhéry with a sports-bodied 40CV. These were undertaken by, among others, Robert Plessier, who was Renault's chief prototype tester, J.A. Garfield, an American engineering colleague of Plessier's and Paul Guillon, head of production at Renault. In May 1925, Garfield and Plessier took the world's one hour and six hours records; in June, the same team with the same car took both the twelve and twenty-four hour world records, the latter despite the need for constant water replenishment owing to a faulty hose clamp. In September, John Duff and Pat Benjafield, 'Bentley Boys' who competed successfully at Le Mans in the 1920s, regained the longer distance record for the British marque, but the shorter remained inviolate. So Renault built a new, slimmer, more streamlined, fabric-bodied coupé with wire-wheels, which, after three attempts, driven by Garfield, Plessier and Guillon, set world records for all distances between 500 and 3,000 miles as well as between 1,000 and 4,000 km and for twenty-four hours (beating the Bentley by over 500 km). This publicity, coupled with the exploits of Renault-engined aircraft, was invaluable to Renault, but as Citroën's car production increased, so Renault's fell, although Renault was producing all sorts of other mechanized vehicles. Something had to be done.

And that something was the 1½-litre six, which brought engine refinement to small cars and although they did not perform, they were smooth. Refinement was emphasized with a three-speed gearbox (with direct top gear) and a torque tube; the magneto gave way to the coil and distributor. The previous six-cylinder cars grew up into eight-cylinder cars and Renaults covered the whole sales gamut.

It was during this decade that credit purchase first gained ground. Louis hated borrowing money and he never did, but he allowed customers to do so in order to buy his wares. DIAC, a Renault subsidiary, was founded in 1924 for this purpose and exists to this very day, although incorporated into Renault Crédit International in 1990.

If the 'Roaring Twenties' were difficult, the 1930s would bring financial problems which would break Renault's most feared rival, but leave him unscathed.

Renault charabanc, 1920. The scene is Parisian, but the designated route is Moroccan, so this twenty-three-seat 3-tonner is probably a new bus ready for export. The French word *char à banc* (car/vehicle with bench/benches) became anglicized into 'sharabang', which described touring coaches, as opposed to single-deckers, which plied set routes and were very popular during the inter-war years. The engine was probably Renault's monobloc 4.5-litre 18CV, petrol unit but the wheels and solid tyres were virtually pre-First World War and the poor driver was still comparatively unprotected.

Renault Type EU Tourer, registered in 1920. In fact, this is a 1917 vehicle splendidly restored and owned by Svenska Renault, Stockholm, in the 1960s; the model actually ceased production in 1918. During restoration, the unavoidable concessions to modern road traffic legislation were incorporated, such as sealed beam headlights within the original lamp housings and discreet black sidelights below. Closely modelled on the Type EK of 1914, the engine was an 80 x 40 mm, 2815cc, monobloc, four-cylinder unit with high tension magneto, cone clutch and four-speed gearbox.

Renault Type HF Torpédo, 1920. It seems likely that this was a six-cylinder (two blocks of three) 40CV machine, possibly even a 1919 Type HD, accurate identification being in doubt because the Billancourt marque changed so slowly at the time and external appearances at the front were similar to those of pre-First World War models. What is certain, though, is that the coachwork was that of an outside company, probably Labourdette, who was fond of the 'flyaway' style of the mudguards and was not averse to experimenting – observe the unusual rear coachwork treatment.

Renault Type EU, 1920. This landaulet was based on a chassis which was first offered in 1917 and ran through to 1921, the engine being a monobloc four-cylinder of 2815cc capacity. It was a development of the 1914 Type EF and was used a great deal in the First World War as a reconnaissance car in torpedo form and as an ambulance, when it was fitted with larger section tyres. This example is elegant yet quite simple, with the traditional folding passenger compartment hood, the coachwork probably being factory manufactured. In appearance it is much like the pre-war vehicles, but it was doubtless more refined.

Renault Type IG-1, 1921. This little sweetie, a three-seater, clover-leaf-type *torpédo* was one of Renault's indestructible, four-cylinder, monobloc, 2120cc, 10CV machines, possibly with a coachbuilt body and probably finished in yellow or cream and black, although, at the time, factory bodies were becoming very fashionable. All Type IGs used the same engine as the famous Type KJ and sported an SEV starter/dynamo, which powered the new-fangled electric lights. It is a left-hand-drive model, still without front wheel brakes and having the rear drum brakes operated either by the right hand lever or right foot pedal.

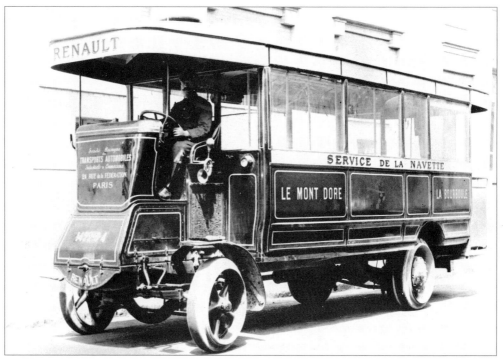

Renault Omnibus, 1922. This was a four-cylinder, 20CV, shaft-drive vehicle, used both as a lorry in various guises, such as a tipper or, as here, a passenger transporter (with the traditional roofed rear platform). The driver sat centrally atop the engine, giving him a commanding view; a *navette* was a shuttle, in this case plying back and forth between the two stated places only. Iron wheels with solid tyres appear to have still been the fashion, doubled on the rear axle, but surely they gave a truly teeth-loosening ride over the Parisian cobblestones.

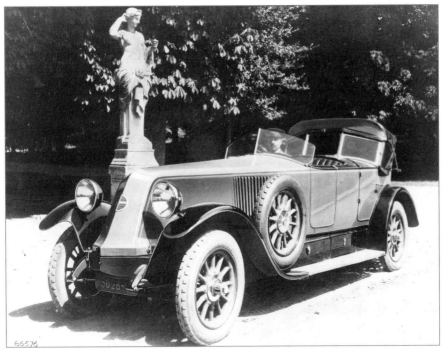

Renault Type JV-1, 1922. This is almost certainly Louis Renault's own 40CV *scaphandrier* ('diving boat'), bearing the registration number 5028-1-2, which first appeared in 1922. But another period photograph shows a swivel handle bonnet catch and a huge (moveable?) search lamp for the chauffeur, not seen on this car. Yet a further known contemporary photograph of the same (?) Kellner 9-litre monster shows much smaller headlights, which appear not to be chromium plated, and there are two small toe kick-plates on the opening body side valences directly below the doors. All three cars have the same number plate.

Renault Type KZ six-wheeler, 1923. During 1923, Louis Renault developed special twin-wheeled versions of the new Type KZ which had both the back axles driving, to respond, by means of wheeled vehicles, to Citroën's trans-Africa publicity stunts with Kégresse half-tracks. The Gradis and Estienne expedition covered the 1,600 km from Colomb-Béchar to Gao in six days, across one of the most dangerous places on earth, the Tanezrouft. Note the absence of mudguards and the use of canvas tops 'to add lightness' and minimize bogging-down, while the tyres are all of an unusual, grippy pattern.

Renault works, Seagrave Road, London, 1924. The nearer cars look new and, as the Renault roundel became a *losange* (diamond) in 1925, the photograph is unlikely to be later. The Types MT and NN looked very similar, but the latter was not commercialized until late in 1924 and the photograph appears to depict a sunny, mid-year scene. The two-seater on the right is probably an earlier Type KJ (all three models used the same engine and had similar sized chassis) and a larger Type NE or NO saloon lurks in the background. Renault finally sold the premises to Rover in the 1930s.

Another view of the large Renault depot in Seagrave Road, Fulham, 1924. One is struck by the still artisanal working methods and the building was probably not constructed for vehicle overhaul as it seems unnecessarily vast and must have been difficult to heat in winter. The mechanic closest to the camera appears to be working on (pre-delivery inspecting?) a new car, probably a little Type KJ 6CV, but he needs to watch that flat tyre. The person standing in the middle distance must be the manager, because he's wearing a trilby and doing nothing!

Renault Type NM-1 Saloon, 1925. M. Repusseau, the French concessionaire for Hartford shock absorbers, started out in this car from Tunis to win the 1925 Monte Carlo Rally and with his passengers took only 150 hours to cover the 4,500 km to the principality. The vehicle is a Weymann-bodied 40CV, with Marchal lamps and centre-lock wire-wheels, carrying heavily patterned balloon tyres. It is a 'cusp' model because the Service des Mines homologated this type on 28 January 1925, four days after the Monte Carlo Rally had finished and yet the car bears the 1925 *losange*, not the 1924 roundel.

Renault Type MC Record Breaker, 1925. On 24 October 1924, the banked track at Montlhéry near Paris was opened. The following 11 May, the vehicle seen here, a normal 40CV Grand Sport with coachwork by Lavocat et Marsaud, devoid of mudguards and lights, attempted some record breaking, but tyre problems and a serious roll put an end to things. A further attempt was made in that month with a similar car, registered 1246 U3, wearing Rudge wire-wheels (perhaps the same car repaired and re-registered?), which took four records and added to these again in June and October, all of which created excellent publicity for Renault.

Renault Type NN Coupé, 1926. Citroën dropped his 5CV in the spring of 1926, so Renault discontinued his rival to that model, his short chassis, clover-leaf Type MT. The Type NN, still using the same little 951cc engine as that model, supplanted it. In March, the up-market models received more enveloping wings, as seen here, and this one appears to be fitted with standard factory coachwork up to the windscreen, whereafter a coachbuilder has constructed a Weymann-type, two-seater, fixed-head coupé with external rear trunk and accompanying spare wheel, which differentiated it from the 'common herd.'

Renault Type MH Six-Wheeler, 1926. As the desert was conquered, so commercial exploitation followed close behind and the Compagnie Générale Transsaharienne, an African freighting organization of which Gradis was a director, was able to open up those commercial routes with the simpler six-wheeler Renaults where Citroën had been unable to proceed earlier with his Kégresse-tracked vehicles for the Compagnie Transafricaine. Renault six-wheelers proliferated, mostly based on modified versions of the 10CV, four-cylinder Type KZ, such as the Type MH, and they were sold worldwide, especially for army use in South America.

Renault Type NN, 1926. In 1924, Renault's little 951cc Type KJ grew up into the Type NN, with a slightly longer wheelbase. Note the left-hand drive and horizontally split windscreen for bad weather driving (no windscreen wipers). This is a Weymann (fabric-bodied) *conduite intérieure luxe* (luxury saloon) manufactured between March 1926, when the curved front mudguards were introduced, and the following October, when the plain diamond badge superseded the Renault roundel. 'Modom', in her cloche hat, button-trimmed silk suit, with fur trimmings and shiny court shoes, is checking the oil, just to show us how user-friendly Renaults had become!

Renault Type NM Record Breaker, 1926. Here exhibited at Beaulieu's National Motor Museum is a replica of Renault's second 40CV 1926 contender, which was created by the late Jackie Pichon (of Clères Motor Museum fame) with his father, who had worked on the original. It used an unsilenced version of the 9.1-litre engine and ran on wire-wheels, and there was a full length 'belly pan' to aid aerodynamics. The thin leathercloth and aluminium body was purpose built and the successful record attempt took place at the Montlhéry banked track near Paris, where Renault undertook many other record attempts for publicity purposes throughout the 1920s and '30s.

Renault Type PG-1 Vivasix, 1927. This was Renault's first 'small' six-cylinder (of 3 litres!), a side-valver with the traditional rear radiator, a three-speed gearbox and a single-plate dry clutch, which improved the driver's lot. This is a factory bodied car with the badge on the lower edge of the coachwork, the extra mudguard-mounted sidelights, the rolled-over front dumb-iron shield and the stepping pad atop the rear mudguard to ease access to the dickey seat. The absence of a star ('stella') above the Renault badge confirms that this is not a de luxe model – despite the windscreen wiper!

Renault Type NM, 1927. The last 40CVs trickled out of the factory in 1927, the final ones bearing the star above the *losange*, and this is probably a factory bodied coupé limousine. The front dumb-irons supported an oil cooler and the chauffeur probably clipped a canvas cover to the ridge at the top of the closed *habitacle* (passenger compartment) and to the top of the eyed windscreen posts in bad weather when an opening windscreen was a necessity without windscreen wipers, even on luxury cars. The artillery type wheels are somewhat *passé*.

Renault Type PG-2 Vivasix, 1928. This is a British right-hand-drive specification car, fitted with a 'Kopolapso' folding hood (in the closed position), the bodywork looking suspiciously like a Weymann fabric type. Note the moveable extra light on the windscreen upright and the absence of the star above the *losange*, thus demoting the car from 'stella' (de luxe) status. The engine was a 3180cc, 16CV side-valver, with either high-tension magneto electrics or coil ignition, coupled to a three-speed gearbox. Perched on its Michelin balloon tyres, it may have rolled serenely along, but it was hardly a flyer.

Renault Type KZ-3 Sportsman's Cabriolet, 1928. Here is one of the two Renaults to start the VIII Monte Carlo Rally, for which the weather turned out to be atrocious and only forty-two of the original sixty-four competitors reached the principality. This 'Etoile du Nord' (Star of the North) is one of the last 'traditional' Renaults, having the radiator behind the engine, and it seems scarcely prepared for the hazards ahead, with its single windscreen wiper, but it does sport a 'super klaxon' on the front bumper and period 'knobblies' (triple-block Dunlop tyres). Perhaps it is not surprising that it was a non-finisher . . .

Renault Type RM Reinastella. 1929. A huge two main-member, four cross-member chassis and a Herculean 7-litre, eight-cylinder engine, with the radiator 'up front' for the first time, was every coachmaker's dream and most of the famous houses tried their hand. The straight-eight composed 2 + 4 + 2 cylinder blocs and the radiator shutters were thermostatically controlled. The car is a very early, factory-bodied, seven-seater limousine, identified by very rounded front mudguards and differing from the 1929 Renahuit in having the diamond badge with the 'stella' above on the prow.

Renault Type KZ-4, 1929. Discreet yet smart and probably photographed in the Bois de Boulogne, such vehicles as this 10CV, four-cylinder omnibus were built for luxury hotel service. Note the non-standard sidelights and that the vehicle is right-hand drive. As this model had no offside passenger door, upon parking the chauffeur could descend promptly and open his rear door with the minimum of delay for his (doubtless important) passengers to alight directly on to the pavement. The following year, the radiator migrated to the front of the engine and the grille bars became vertical.

CHAPTER FOUR

L'AUTOMOBILE DE FRANCE

Caudron-Renault C362 Rafale Record Holder, 1933. By 1930, Renault was the world's largest aero engine manufacturer, but courted publicity to counteract Citroën's and Peugeot's competition. Renault was Caudron's major aero-engine supplier and took a majority holding in the ailing company; immediately, Renault produced the Bengali, a 6-litre, 165bhp, inverted-four engine, which, in the new C362 Rafale, came second (to an 8-litre, 207bhp Potez 53) in the 1933 Coupe Deutsch de la Meurthe, the most prestigious air race of the era. It later broke the light aircraft record for 1,000 km at 328kph and 100 km at 344kph. Racing Caudron-Renault planes became virtually supreme in the 1930s.

INTRODUCTION

In 1929, for the 1930 model year, Renault introduced a radical change to his cars, the repositioning of the radiator in front of the engine. The constant rise in engine output had revealed the thermal shortcomings of the traditional rear-located radiator and finned flywheel Renault layout.

Another – non-technical – innovation was the adoption of model names, rather than model numbers (shades of the 1990s?). The names Mona, Viva, Nerva and Reina saw the decade in, suffixed with – in the standard model – the number of the cylinders, thus Monaquatre (the small-capacity, four-cylinder vehicle) or Vivaquatre (the medium-capacity, four-cylinder vehicle); this latter was available as a six-cylinder, thus Vivasix, and, for any of the models, the suffix 'stella' was added to denote deluxe versions, in place of the number of cylinders, so Monastella or Vivastella. As of 1929, there were also the small capacity, eight-cylinder Nervastella and the large capacity, eight-cylinder vehicles, firstly misnamed Renahuit, then Reinahuit and, finally, Reinastella (because it was the top-of-the-range model). Later came Celta (confusingly also having a Celtastandard version), Nova and Juva, as well as additional names such as 'Sport' or 'Grand Sport', thus Viva Grand Sport, for example – all rather confusing, except to the initiated. Left-hand-drive cars became predominant.

By 1934, aerodynamics were playing an increasingly important role in vehicle design. On everyday Renault models, the wheels were either plain or perforated or had simple covers, while radiator grilles sloped ever more backwards with headlamps huddled up close by. For the Paris Show of that year, Renault unveiled a *hyperaérodynamique* (super dynamic), six-cylinder Vivastella Grand Sport with heavily raked, shield-shaped, vertically barred radiator grille, low leading-edge front mudguards, with large, low, inset headlamps, sloped windscreen, wire-wheels with rear spats, no running boards and rounded, sloping tail. It was a remarkable vehicle which grew up into the eight-cylinder Nervastella and, eventually, into the Nervastella Grand Sport.

This design, albeit with modified wheels, remained unaltered until the Paris show of 1936, when the 'Ford front' came in; this was an inverted triangular grille, vertically ridged down the centre and with vertical bars. The headlights were enclosed inside integral fairings, somewhat on the top of the front mudguards, but protected by a teardrop-shaped glass front; the horizontal bonnet side vents were changed, but the remainder of the bodywork, whether saloon, convertible or coupé, remained unchanged.

Another significant signpost was the introduction in 1937 of Renault's first chassis-less car, the Juvaquatre, an Opel Kadett lookalike, in which the chassis, with side- and cross-members made from pressed sheet steel, was welded together with flat, sheet steel to form the floor. It had a new side-valve, 1-litre engine and, in van form, lingered on until 1960, albeit with a more modern engine.

In 1934, Renault continued breaking records with a Riffard-designed, fully streamlined, wire-wheeled, eight-cylinder Nervasport, which took the forty-eight hours target at over 100mph. With over 40,000 aero engines produced, Renault powered all the major makers' planes, including Latécoère (later the Aéropostale, the premier air post company), which flew all over the world. Renault bought up the famous, but unstable, Caudron company (complete with aerodynamicist, Marcel Riffard) and, as well as winning the famous Coupe Deutsch de la Meurthe with a Caudron-Renault C460 (first three places in 1934, first four places in 1935 and winning again in 1936), took the world air speed record in 1934 with a 370hp-engined plane at over 505kph (from a 1000hp US racing plane). At the famous 1935 Los Angeles Air Show, the same 8-litre plane beat all other planes up to 9 litres (in the Greve Trophy) and then all-comers of unlimited capacity in the Thompson Trophy, having overtaken almost every other competitor. The Americans were so incredulous that they insisted on scrutineering the plane (despite a Veritas Bureau Certificate), which merely confirmed the unbelievable. The ensuing prestige for Renault was immeasurable. Air companies all over the world started to use Renault engines and such pilots as Boucher, Détroyat, Delmotte, Mermoz and Bastie, from aviation's hall of fame, broke records everywhere with Renault-powered aircraft.

But political polarization was sweeping across Europe – Fascism rose in Italy, Spain and Germany and was widespread in France and the United Kingdom. Amazingly, 1936 saw 60,000 Renault vehicles produced out of a French total of 204,000, despite a bitter and prolonged strike by occupying workers closing the factory completely from 28 May to 14 June. The action started because the Popular Front had agreed a forty-hour working week with paid holidays. Louis was so caught off balance that he appointed François Lehideux, the son-in-law of his late brother, Fernand, to negotiate a settlement, the first time he had handed over power to anyone else. But after the settlement, he took on 5,000 new workers to prepare his forthcoming cars.

This manoeuvre led to deep resentment among the workers and compounded the existing ill-feeling that Louis had not bailed André Citroën out of bankruptcy in 1934, just as the famous Citroën T/A was launched. Louis had made his adversary envious by showing him around Billancourt, which had taken him twenty-five years to develop; this had so impressed Citroën that he razed the Quai de Javel to the ground and, within two years, tried to rebuild it in competition, which contributed considerably to the ruination of his company. Louis also counter-boxed Citroën's every smart manoeuvre – a typical one being his introduction of his own 'SA' (*suspension amorti* – controlled movement) engined versions of the Vivaquatre, in reply to Citroën's '*moteur flottant*' (floating engine), for which they had to pay significant fees to the original licence holders.

But Louis' tricks were to cost him dear.

Renault Type RM Reinastella Cabriolet, 1930. This is a last example in the 1930 horizontally slatted radiator series, which disappeared in October of the year, and the small badge with star above encourages that conclusion. The solidity of the conception indicates either Hibbard et Darrin or Kellner as the coachmaker, but the contrasting waist-band and the wheel embellishers have a touch of Million-Guiet about them. What is certain is that there are six cylinders totalling 7 litres capacity of stump-pulling torque under that imposing prow.

Renault Type RM Reinastella Sportsman's Coupé, 1930. With the huge seven-litre engine and rock-solid chassis, these top-of-the-range cars could carry virtually any bodywork and this is a Weymann coupé with a touch of Bugatti about it probably in mustard yellow and black. The small badge and star, just visible above the light at the front, again indicate 1930 model before the salon changes (vertical radiator slats) were introduced on this model. Points of interest are the coach-like door handles and the transfer of the twin spare wheels to the rear – to help traction perhaps?

Renault Type RY-2 Monastella, 1930. Basically, this saloon was the same as the Monasix, a 1496cc, six-cylinder 8CV, with three-speed gearbox, originating in September 1926 when the radiator was still behind the engine. The Type RY-2 was the first version of this model to have the radiator at the front, protected by a horizontally barred grille. The Monastella was distinguished by chromium-plated road-wheel embellishers and sidelights protruding either side of the front bulkhead, the one seen here having factory built coachwork. Top speed was just above 60mph and servo brakes were fitted.

Renault Type RM Reinastella, 1932. This is Louis Renault's personal car, which is actually a 1929 Type BM-1, bodied by Kellner as a *torpédo 'scaphandrier'* to look like a 1932 Type RM-3, which had a front radiator with an appropriate grille. The special *roues* Rudge and newer lamps are attention distracters from the older front bulkhead. The original engine was an eight-cylinder, but the production car had a six-cylinder, 7-litre unit with a four-speed (overdrive top) gearbox; it is unlikely that *le patron* would have countenanced a standard power plant, so this car was probably 'quite fast'.

Renault Type RM-3 Reinastella, 1932. Looking as if it were machined from the solid, this is a typical Renault 'large barge' for those who had not lost their shirts in the Wall Street crash. This chassis with bespoke coachwork (very often by Kellner) was used by the presidents of France at the time and, although this is probably a factory coachbuilt running on Michelin tyres, they were almost invariably right-hand drive and sported twin flat-blade bumpers. The 7-litre, eight cylinder engine produced 110bhp and the slightly inclined radiator surround and bonnet side doors (*volets*) enable us to date this car to within a few months.

Renault Type YN-2 Monaquatre, 1933. One of the second series of this type, having the distinguishing straight bumpers at the front and the little doors along the bonnet sides, this factory model was introduced at the October 1933 Paris Salon replacing the very similar Type YN-1, of which there were three series and only the last having the bonnet doors. It was built up to January 1933, when the 'aerodynamic' saloons superseded them and it was powered by a 1463cc, 8CV, four cylinder, side-valve engine. Despite its barn door shape, it could reach 65mph.

nault Type YN-3 Monaquatre, 1934. Introduced in 1932, the Monaquatre boasted a side-valve, 1.3-litre (later 1.5-litre) r-cylinder engine, with conventional electric starting; the following year, aerodynamics demanded a new sloping iator. The vertical slats on the bonnet sides were replaced with three little opening doors and the straight-bladed mpers gained a dip in the centre. For the standard, factory bodied cabriolet illustrated, the 34bhp at 3500rpm engine s linked to a gearbox on which second and top had synchromesh.

Renault Type ZG-4 Nervasport, 1934. The main difference between this Nervasport '80' and the later (March 1935 onwards) Type ADG-1 '85' Nervasport was the engine's stroke – 80 as opposed to 85mm. No 51, Lahaye and Quatresous, won the XIVe Rallye Monte Carlo in January 1935, so probably used the older car. Compare this winner to Repusseau's 40CV, 1925 Monte Carlo Rally winner and the knobbly tyres and phalanx of *lampes anti-brouillard et longue portée* (fog and driving lamps) show how much more seriously the event was taken later on. Then, as now, *noblesse oblige* and suits were *de rigueur* for the trophy winners.

Renault Nervasport Record Breaker, 1934. This car was based on the eight-cylinder Type ZC-4, a development of t
Type ZC-1 of 1933; among the records it captured in April 1934 was the world forty-eight hours at over 100mph. T
steering wheel was slightly centred from the normal offset to achieve the streamlined *monoplace* (single-seate
coachwork, but the chassis was standard and the eight exhaust stubs have certainly 'coloured' the bodywork. The drive
included Fromentin, Wagner, Berthelon and Quatresous, the 1935 Monte Carlo Rally winner (with a Rena
Nervasport). The (then) astonishing shape was widely reproduced as a toy car at the time.

Renault Type ZC-4 Nervasport, 1935. At the 1934 Paris Salon in October this model, seen here in Renault's Champ
Elysées showroom in its drophead cabriolet version, was introduced for the 1935 model year. It had the same eig
cylinder, 28CV, 4827cc, side-valve engine from the ZC-1 introduced in September 1933, coupled to a three-spe
gearbox – an imposing vehicle by any standards, with large headlamps, solid-spoked steel-wheels and a foldab
windscreen. Interior finish was luxurious by contemporary standards, but the aftermath of the Depression, the rise
Fascism and monetary uncertainties contributed to a short life for this final model in the ZC series.

Renault Type ACX-1 Viva Grand Sport, 1935. Presented at the October 1934 Paris Salon, it retained the two-piece front bumper, the only revision for the following year being a one-piece, drop-centre item. Available in five versions as well as a bare (de luxe) chassis, this *conduite intérieure grand luxe six places* (luxury six-seater saloon) lived up to its name and is seen standing on open land (now completely built over) adjoining Renault's then recently re-occupied Acton HQ on Western Avenue (in the background), which was still a single carriageway main road. Observe the anachronistic wooden lookalike steel wheels.

Renault Type ZR-2 Celtaquatre, 1935. This saloon had a very short production life between March 1935, when it superseded the Type ZR-1, and September of that year, when it was itself superseded by the Type ADC-1. The difference between the ZR types was that the earlier one had three opening doors along each side of the bonnet. With wire-wheels, it was sold in the UK as the 'Airsport' and this particular example has been in the same family from new, the first owner running it until 1969. It was completely restored in the 1970s, but now lies deteriorating in a country garage.

Renault Type AEB-2 Juvaquatre, 1937. This is one of the pre-series cars in de luxe version, about forty of which were sent out through the network and abroad for in-field evaluation and fault finding, among which were flimsy bumpers, too thin a steering-wheel rim, frequent loss of tune and poor cold-weather starting. Production corrections further included wind-up windows and longitudinal grille bars. Note that this is a front-hinged, two-door version (four doors – centre hinged – came later) with external spare wheel (internalized on post-war models to prevent theft).

Renault Type BCX-3 Viva Grand Sport, 1938. Slow sales of large cars in the late 1930s meant annual changes were minimal. The Type BCX-1, commercialized in March 1937, superseded the Type ACX-3, but was externally distinguishable only by its straight bumpers and overriders (previously dip-centre type). In October 1937 at the Paris Salon, the 1938 Type BCX-2 was identical but for the absence of the rear wheel spats, which were replaced for the 1938 Type BCX-3 (seen here) in April 1938 – very confusing. This one retained the vertical grille bars, so cannot be confused with the nearly identical one on p. 62, which has horizontal grille bars.

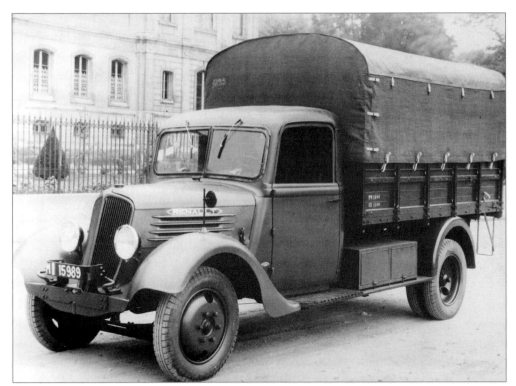

Renault Type AGC Lorry, 1938. Old habits die hard and the controversy between forward-control and standard-control cabs raged throughout the 1930s. Renault backed both horses and manufactured both types, this French military version, complete with wing mirror, being typical of the 'older' (conventional?) generation. Almost certainly it was powered by Renault's old '85' petrol war-horse, but it already had front-hinged cab doors, while retaining the 'inverted claphands' windscreen wipers. Any remaining examples were doubtless commandeered by the German forces for war work.

enault Type BDF-1 Primaquatre, 1938. The factory bodywork was identical for the 8CV Types ADC-2 and ADC-3 'eltaquatre and the more powerful Types ACL-2 and BDF-1 Primaquatre. These solid, dependable family saloons, though technically and dynamically inferior to the contemporary Citroën 'traction', sold steadily in many markets. enault in London had sales right for the colonies, so, to satisfy 'Empire-made' requirements, they assembled cars at cton with a considerable British content (wheels, tyres, electrics, lights, bumpers, etc.). This is a British-assembled car ith Firestone (not Renault) tyres and the Renault losange on the wheel hub caps.

Renault Type AEB-2 Juvaquatre, 1939. The resemblance of the contemporary Opel Kadett to this rare Grand Luxe fixed head coupé is clear. Unusual bodywork apart, the chromed *enjoliveurs* (wheel embellishers), chromed bumper overriders, chromed rear number-plate light, parking light, clumsily mounted semaphore indicators and beige steering wheel all betoken 'grand luxe' specification, but the car's wheels sport hub plates with the name RENAULT at the centre (normally plain), which might suggest a car especially prepared for a motor show. The 1003cc, side-valve engine and three-speed gearbox were carried over from the 1938 model.

Renault Type BCX-3 Viva Grand Sport, 1939. This vehicle is a 'cusp year' model, for it has headlights in the integral wing housing of a 1938 model (the later models had separate housings), it has the horizontal grille bars of a 1939 model, but the front windows have no swivelling quarter lights, a feature of that year's models and, of course, the Lucas foglights and AA badge are non-standard! It was originally sold to an English nobleman and, after a period in the North Country, is now believed to be in Wales awaiting restoration.

CHAPTER FIVE

REVOLUTION

Billancourt works, 1945. Louis Renault had no alternative to save his factory's machinery and workers from being transshipped to Germany than to work for the Nazis. For this 'collaboration', the Renault factories and those of other 'collaborators' were bombed, not too accurately, by the Allies half a dozen times. As a result, there were many distant civilian casualties and up to 80 per cent of the Billancourt factory was left in ruins at the time of the August 1944 Paris liberation. Louis was never to see his beloved works revitalized and flourishing again, for he was dead and buried before October was out.

INTRODUCTION

Louis Renault had fought long and hard to build up his enterprise from an artisanal garden workshop to be the most powerful, privately owned company in France. Once before, he had turned his factories over to the manufacture of fighting materials, but this time he was reluctant to let his country, *l'Empire de Billancourt*, go to war because the scenario was different.

This time, he was not thirty-seven with the focused energy of a man ten years younger; he was approaching retirement and was exhausted. This time there were no *Taxis de la Marne* and a General Galliéni to save Paris from the Panzer-mounted Germans as they outflanked the Maginot Line and crushed a disorganized France. And Louis was no politician. He believed that a peace agreement could be hammered out between the Germans, the French and the British, so he continued to produce the Juvaquatre and other civilian vehicles. On the orders of the Minister of Armaments, Louis, with his wife, Christiane, and his son, Jean-Louis, was sent on a mission to America in June 1940, leaving the factory in the hands of François Lehideux. In July, when he returned, his beloved Billancourt was under German control. He was dumbfounded.

After a violent argument with the scheming Lehideux, he took back the running of his empire. As Jean-Louis was presently too young, Louis had hoped that Lehideux would inherit his domain on merit, but his nephew had been manoeuvring secretly to gain control of the Renault empire and Louis could not forgive such treachery. Lehideux managed to have himself appointed as 'Executive Director of the Committee of the Organization of French Car Manufacturers', a grouping demanded by the Germans, so that they could control that industry; this position was ideal for Lehideux to interfere with Renault. Louis felt ill and totally isolated.

His sole aim was to get Billancourt working again, but the Nazis insisted that he should only manufacture lorries for the Wehrmacht. Louis could not cope with this situation; he ceased his habit of patrolling his factory and locked himself in his office to do nothing. Meanwhile, Charles-Edmond Serre, who had been with Louis since the turn of the century, and his assistant, Fernand Picard, who had come to Billancourt from Delage in 1935, dreamed of a cheap-to-produce, economical-to-run small car for the lean post-war years.

The Germans ordered various work to be carried out, which was delayed by sabotage and strikes; they threatened to strip the factory and transport all the machinery and workers (as forced labour) to Germany. To avoid this, Louis was obliged to confirm that the work was to be done and some of it was completed eventually, with lengthy delays and huge 'losses' of raw materials. It was a game of cat and mouse, with Louis always playing for time. The Allies' planes targeted Louis' factories several times for this 'collaboration'.

Despite an absolute prohibition on prototypes, new models were cobbled together secretly; a handful of scaled-down American lookalikes, about Primaquatre size (11CV/1800cc), and an unusual slab-fronted, two-door, rear-engined concoction, looking nothing like any other Renault before it.

By February 1944, Louis was very ill; his speech was indistinct and he could no longer write or draw. In May, the factory was closed for a fortnight because there was no electricity and in July because there was no work. Like a sleepwalker, Louis shuffled through his silent factories and remained mute whenever he met his colleagues. In August, Paris was liberated. A month later, 'Emperor Louis' was imprisoned in Fresnes on charges of collaboration and he died on 24 October 1944. How he died is still an open question; the official verdict was 'cerebral circulatory complications', but rumours of blows, administered to his neck by persons unknown, still persist and it is a mystery which no one seems really interested to solve, after all these years.

Prior to Renault's death the state had already appointed a provisional administrator of his factories. At forty-six, a doctor-at-law and a renowned Resistance fighter, Pierre Lefaucheux was a Renault enthusiast who had a Viva Grand Sport, but he was faced with a formidable task. He tested the 4CV (which, after secret comparative tests at his Herqueville estate, Louis had rejected in favour of the 'American' Primalégère) and decided to proceed with its development, but, because his height made entry into the rear of the car difficult, he specified four doors.

On 16 January 1945, Régie Nationale des Usines Renault (RNUR) came into being, a state enterprise endowed with all Louis' business assets worldwide (aside from his personal possessions, which were immense) but free to act as a non-governmental entity. The factory purges continued, but Lefaucheux did not lose sight of his target. He abandoned the 11CV in favour of the 4CV, to be built 'at 300 per day from July 1949!' He was thought to be completely mad, but he went to fight the government to have Renault permitted to manufacture cars.

The government invited Dr Ferdinand Porsche, then a prisoner under surveillance in France, to give his opinion on the car; Lefaucheux was furious with this interference and wrote to the minister responsible in no uncertain terms. It was all a storm in a teacup, for Dr Porsche made a few minor detailed comments for possible improvements during the nine meetings which he had with the French specialists, but, in fact, no alterations were made (despite what certain Porsche historians have written . . .).

The 4CV was shown to the press in September 1946 and to the public at the following Paris Salon, although there were, as yet, no lines on which to produce it. Meanwhile RNUR manufactured over 8,000 vehicles in that year, mostly GMC trucks refurbished under contract to the US forces, but also many of their own commercials and five Juvaquatres. The 'flea' was officially launched at the 1947 Paris Show and simultaneously in 300 towns and cities across France. Success – and the inevitable black market – was instantaneous. Lefaucheux attained his sales target: 300 a day by 1949 and 500 a day by 1954. With the democratization of motor sport, the sporting potential of the 4CV shone; Jean Rédélé, the father of Alpine, was pre-eminent among many outstanding 4CV competitors. The car's first major class win was in the 1949 Monte Carlo Rally and others soon followed.

'The little pat of butter' set Renault back on its commercial feet and France back on wheels.

Renault Type AGR Lorry, 1940. This 4-ton, forward-control vehicle, built under German orders for the Wehrmacht, betrays its pre-war ancestry by its bow front. Strangely, it does not wear masks over the lights, but bars are fitted to the rear quarter-lights for security reasons. A tiny Renault *losange* surmounts the radiator, but Louis could not have been very proud of this. The engine was an 85 x 120 mm four-cylinder petrol unit and the older rim-fixing road wheels were still employed.

Renault Type AGK Truck, 1941. This forward-control, bow-fronted 6-tonner, one of the last of the pre-war-designed commercials, was manufactured for military purposes until the Type AH series came in. Note the rear-hinged cab door, no brightwork or external mirrors and pendant parallel windscreen wipers which had replaced the 'inverted claphands' type. The step and external grab-handle-aided cab entry and crescent lower screens improved forward vision. The cab is similar to the classic pre-war 15-tonner Type ADTD, which boasted a six-cylinder direct-injection diesel engine and five-speed gearbox.

The Renault war effort, 1942. No, this not a machine shop reconditioning Juvaquatre engines, but personnel at Renault UK's Acton factory, engaged in building and overhauling multi-cylinder marine engines for the British Admiralty during the Second World War. In 1935, the English company had re-occupied their Acton works so when supplies from France of the Renault vehicles, which they assembled for the British Empire, petered out in 1940 it needed alternative work. Thanks to the perspicacity of the then managing director, Noel Martin, the remaining workers were quickly and usefully employed on this type of essential war work throughout the conflict.

Renault 4CV 106-E1 Prototype No. 1, 1943. This unusual hand-built prototype was the original Renault 4CV, looking completely unlike any previous Renault, having all-round independent suspension, hydraulic brakes, rear engine/gearbox ensemble and unitary construction, which would be retained while other major revisions would be incorporated. The front was modified and lowered, with the headlights moved in line with the wheels, the windscreen was enlarged, four doors (eventually) replaced the two and were B-pillar-hinged and the rear wing cooling slots were modified. Note the headlights bearing blackout masks, the semaphore indicators preceding the doors and the curious 'Louis Renault' emblems adorning the wheel hub caps.

Renault Type AHN Truck, 1943. This forward-control, flat-fronted, 3½-ton truck was one of the three manufactures permitted to Renault from July 1941, the others being the Type AHS 2-tonner and the 6C125 marine engine. The lorries were for Wehrmacht use and the cab script indicates 3,300 kilos unladen weight and 3,500 kilos maximum permitted carried weight. Note the modified diamond motif and unusual axle deflection capabilities. Such ongoing manufacture for the Axis powers attracted RAF air raids on Billancourt in March 1943, which caused much damage in the factory as well as outside. Used for civilian purposes after the war, it went out of production in 1946.

Renault 4CV 106-E2 Prototype No. 2, 1943. One can see shades of Issigonis' (later) Morris Minor (particularly around the non-suicide doors) on this second attempt (one of forty) to finalize a new economical family saloon for Renault's post-war range. The same general layout was employed for this prototype, as had been used for the first effort, except that the windows were sliding ones. The third version looked very like the final car and Pierre Lefaucheux decided that this would be Renault's big break, but manufacture would have to be on an unprecedented scale. He aimed high and pushed hard and the rest of the 4CV story has gone down in motoring history.

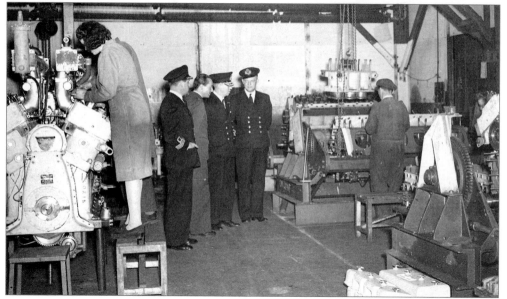

Renault war effort, 1944. Renault were awarded some war-work contracts with the Admiralty and here the 'top brass' are seen on a visit to the works. One of the contracts was for assembling, testing, disassembling, re-assembling and final testing of twelve-cylinder, 500 hp, V12 marine diesel engines of the Type TPM. These units would have been a tight fit into Juvaquatres of the era and HM Factory Inspector would suffer a cardiac arrest nowadays if he found the workers on the left perched on a rickety stool all day long . . . but this is how the British company survived during the hostilities and the works were not bombed, unlike Billancourt.

Renault war work, 1944. Empowering women is not a new phenomenon, as these Renault factory workers at Acton clearly demonstrate. The bands are emery cloths, one of which a worker is holding in tension with the pulley polisher, being turned by the flexible drive from the electric motor in the right foreground of the photograph. Some of the crankshaft journals for this marine engine have already been individually polished and each would then have had the main and big-end bearings hand-lapped for maximum service, all of which is now done automatically by robots in an enclosed environment.

Mr Noel Martin. This gentleman was the managing director of Renault in the United Kingdom from 1941 until 1951. He must have been well connected in the engineering business, for he secured contract repair work for the company from the War Office to repair ships' engines, which became the mainstay of the company's business, these contracts continuing until well after the cessation of hostilities. This was essential to the firm's survival because nothing was available from Renault in France for assembly. Despite the French export push post-war, any vehicles which became available had to be assembled and re-exported 'to the British Empire' to earn foreign exchange.

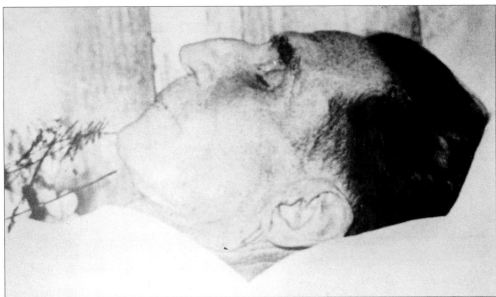

Louis Renault, born 12 February 1877, died 24 October 1944, lies ready for the journey to his final resting place in a small cemetery at Herqueville. Convinced that it would be proven that he had collaborated with the Nazis under duress to avoid large-scale deportation of his workers to Germany, his openness had been rewarded with a treacherous arrest, wrongful imprisonment and a mysterious death, in which an indifferent French bureaucracy and ineffective legal system colluded under sustained left-wing political pressure in the tumultuous aftermath of war. After his death, the charges of collaboration were conveniently dropped. One wonders what less compromising decisions a Sir William Lyons or a Lord Nuffield might have taken when faced with similar insoluble problems . . .

Renault Type BFK-2 Juvaquatre, 1947. Many people think that *la Régie*'s first car was the 4CV; in a sense it was, because earlier cars which it manufactured were Louis Renault-inspired pre-war designs, which had to continue in production until the 4CV assembly lines could be created. Renault's stop-gap car mainstay was this Juvaquatre, of which some thousands were built up to July 1948. The production line is seen here in 1947. (The cars have four doors and there are chrome embellishers at the bottom trailing corner of the rear door windows, both identification points for post-war cars.)

Renault's Billancourt works, 1947. As a result of the bombings by both the RAF and the USAF, Billancourt was about 80 per cent destroyed and a huge amount of work was required to clear the rubble before serious manufacture could start again. And while the clearing up proceeded, the manufacture started again slowly, with sheets closing off those parts where the new production lines could be installed. This picture illustrates graphically the difficulties which had to be overcome before production of the new 4CV could begin in earnest. And yet it all took place without Louis . . .

Renault Type AHN-1 Dropside Lorry, 1947. Comparing this commercial with the same model manufactured for military purposes four years earlier, there had not been many changes: what had been a war-horse for Louis continued as a beast of burden for *la Régie*. Motive power for this 3½-tonner was a six-cylinder petrol engine and there were servo-assisted brakes and rim-fixing wheels. The platform's Renault-bediamonded metal drop-sides advertised the maker unmistakably, in the same way that the tailboard on many commercials was to do for other makers, decades later.

Renault Type BFK-4 Juvaquatre,1947. Renault's pre-war Opel Kadett lookalike was updated with four doors and hydraulic brakes, all-round ifs by transverse springs, 1003cc side-valve engine and unitary body to continue the pre-war formula until 1948. Starting in 1937, about 40,000 saloons were sold in all, but the *break* (estate car) and van with the 4CV's ohv engine from 1953 and finally with the Dauphine's version from 1956 – hence the new name 'Dauphinoise' soldiered on, until the advent of the Four in 1961. Examples could still be found in use in rural France in the 1980s.

Renault 4CV, 1947. These are R-1060 *normale* saloons being loaded for export, but to where is not known. The nearest car has the rear number-plate light on the end of the bodywork, on to which the number plate was painted directly; the separate rear *immatriculation* (registration number) and the wing-mounted rear lights (a single offside item on the *commerciale*) were introduced for the 1950 models at the October 1949 Paris Salon. The flat roof of the early model can be seen clearly, as the *toit bombé* (domed roof), giving the extra interior headroom, did not appear until October 1948.

Renault Type AHG-2 Juva Van, 1948. At the end of 1948, the Juvaquatre saloon was phased out because the 4CV came on stream. Renault needed a small *commerciale*, but could not build the Juva van in-house, so body shells were pressed by Chausson (who also produced some Frégate panels) and assembled by Renault alongside the 4CV. In 1951, the van was given side windows, which model then became the only one available. In 1954, it gained the 747cc ohv engine from the 4CV and in 1956 the Dauphine's 845cc version and a new rear door and a new name – Dauphinoise. Production ceased in 1960.

Renault Project 108, 1948. Having first launched the 4CV, Lefaucheux sought to attract a wider clientele and so with this experience the design office were able to assemble this steel-bodied prototype, a six-seater with longitudinal rear engine *over* the column change-controlled four-speed gearbox driving the rim-fixing rear wheels. The early tests in spring 1948 revealed that the good shape (Cx 0.29) permitted a top speed of 130kph, but there were engine overheating problems. Surprisingly, the layout did not allow sufficient interior room and the project was abandoned in favour of a crash programme, which led to the classically laid-out Frégate.

Renault Project 108, 1948. Another view of the first 'big car' experiment to be tackled by *la Régie*'s development department and showing some of the problems that faced them, such as the (eventually insurmountable) cooling difficulties in spite of the huge, ugly air scoops in front of the rear wheels. The 4CV-like rear window offers poor three-quarter vision, as it is forced to be too high because of the overall height of the engine sitting above the gearbox, and the requisite access thereto. A huge amount of space is lost lengthwise near the tail end, meaning, unfortunately, it was a no-goer fairly early on.

CHAPTER SIX

ECONOMIC RECOVERY

*Sisters in the metal. But for the rally plaques celebrating
Renault's centenary in May 1998, this could well have been a
period Renault publicity photograph from the 1950s when
Renault really set France back on its motoring feet. On the left
is a 1952 4CV Convertible and the lighter-coloured car is a
standard 1958 Dauphine with whitewall tyres, both framed by
the famous Renault arch, which leads into the garden square,
where Louis' original shed still stands. In front of that
monument stands a decaying Renault FT-17 Light Tank while
the Renault directorial office block presides over it.*

INTRODUCTION

While the 4CV sold strongly for *la Régie* throughout this decade, other cars played their commercial part: the Juva *break* (later 'Dauphinoise'), the Colorale range and the Frégate were there, as well as the Dauphine from 1956 onwards, together with an impressive range of commercial vehicles.

The Colorale range (COLOniale + ruRALE) was a doughty slogger with the old pre-war '85' (from its 85 mm bore) side-valve petrol engine and rear-wheel drive all carried on a separate chassis; it served the rural and taxi trade well, but unspectacularly. Inheritor of the Frégate's ohv engine in 1952, it was used for many long-distance publicity treks (Tierra del Fuego/Alaska, Montigueux/Himalayas, etc.), before disappearing from Renault's catalogue at the end of the decade.

In 1947, wanting to broaden the company's sales potential, Lefaucheux had ordered the study of a rear-engined 2-litre (Project 108); the prototype was tested in 1949, but was abandoned the following year because of insurmountable difficulties. The launch date was to be retained (Paris Salon, 1951), so the pressure was on. Meanwhile the Korean War broke out so, to avoid a forthcoming governmental embargo due on new cars (effective from 1 January 1951), the Frégate was launched on 30 November 1950, although it was not properly developed. It boasted all-round coil-spring suspension (unusual at the time) and the engine, based on 4CV principles (wet-liner, ohv), was somewhat underpowered. It drove to the rear wheels through a four-piece transmission shaft to a differential bolted to the underside of the flat floor, which was costly and suffered significant wear. It was no real challenge to Citroën's T/A, but it gave Renault a presence in the same market sector. A lacklustre reputation was little improved either by successive power increases or by the 'Transfluide' (semi-automatic gearbox) version or yet by the Domaine or Manoir *break* variants. Like its sister, the Frégate sought publicity through record-breaking (Lapland to Cape of Good Hope in the summer of 1958) but, after 170,000 examples, production ceased.

Unfortunately, Lefaucheux was killed in February 1955; he was driving a special Frégate with a more powerful engine and lightweight panels when it hit black ice near St Dizier and the car left the road, the driver being freakishly killed by a blow to the nape of his neck from his own briefcase, lying loose on the rear seat. The factory's mourning mirrored that accorded to Marcel Renault half a century earlier after the fateful Paris–Madrid carnage.

Pierre Dreyfus succeeded Pierre Lefaucheux and had much to do. First, he finished the creation of SAVIEM, the heavy vehicle division of RNUR, uniting Latil, SOMUA and Renault as a powerful commercial vehicle combine. He had endorsed the testing of Project 109, originally commenced in 1952 and aptly named Corvette; publicly launched in 1955 as the Dauphine, it was Renault's *coup de foudre* (thunderbolt) for the

1950s. Mechanically and in terms of suspension, it was a grown-up 4CV, clothed in svelte coachwork, recalling much of the Frégate's rounded symmetry and sold at a very competitive price, with most of the extras as standard (heater, demister, steering lock, underseal, two-tone horns, automatic choke, child-proof door locks, etc.). Within days of its launch, there was a huge waiting list and it was quickly successful in competition.

Amédée Gordini, the Italian-born Frenchman who had constructed and run his eponymous racing cars, could no longer survive financially and became contracted as a consultant to *la Régie*. Promptly he created the Gordini-Dauphine, which produced 25 per cent more power via a new cylinder head with inclined valves, a large carburettor and a free-flow exhaust. With an extra ratio in the three-speed gearbox, the car's impressive record grew: class wins in the 1956, 1957, 1958 and 1959 Mille Miglia, outright winner of the 1958 Monte Carlo Rally and the 1956, 1958 and 1962 Tour de Corse, touring class overall winner and runner-up in the 1959 Liège–Rome–Liège (45 minutes ahead of the opposition), class winner in the 1960 and 1962 Neige et Glace Rally, etc.

Undergoing 6,000 automatic checks during manufacture and being made on (Renault) transfer machines, a finished Dauphine came off the new Flins factory production line every 30 seconds! Daily manufacture rose from 1,000 units to 1,400 and then to 1,600 – unseen hitherto in France; by early 1960, over a million had been made, of which half had been exported. It was selling more quickly than Volkswagen's Beetle in the USA; it was assembled by Alfa Romeo in Italy and in countries far and wide – Belgium, England, Australia, Japan, Spain, South Africa, Brazil, Mexico and more. It was *the* chic small car to be seen in and it rode so serenely and quietly that it was frequently 'overdriven' in the wrong places, thus earning it an undeserved reputation for poor handling. Its economy became a benchmark. The famous from all over the world came to watch the production of the little marvel – Elizabeth of England, the Rainiers from Monaco and Kruschev from Russia, to name but a few.

Neither was Renault finished with record breaking. In 1956 at Salt Lake, USA, *l'étoile filante* ('Shooting Star'), a gas turbine streamliner, using a 270CV Turbomeca power unit and driven by Jean Hébert, broke and still holds the world's speed record for turbine cars at 309kph.

Lefaucheux had not been slow to let the Renault workers share in the company's profitable progress; there was an agreement to link earnings to the cost of living, as well as rises for working efficiency. Three weeks' paid holiday became everyone's entitlement and the fund for pensioners at sixty-five was increased. Again Renault led the field.

But while things were going well for Renault and new ideas were being brought to fruition, the United States, a huge export market for the Dauphine, was becoming fragile and from that sobering adventure Dreyfus and his army learned a bitter lesson.

Renault Colorale Prairie, 1950. Long before Volksford's Sharaxy or Fiageot's Ulyeightohsix, before Renault's Matra-inspired Espace or American or Japanese people vans, before Ford or Bedford conversions or Volkswagen's Microbus or even Fiat's Multipla, Renault had already invented the MPV with their five-door Prairie, seating four to six people on two bench seats (the rear one also folded forward) and even a seventh on a crossways *strapontin* (folding seat) at the back. The rear door had a top-hinged windowed upper half and a right-hand-hinged lower half. Commercial and taxi derivatives with alternative accessing, canvas sides, platform rear and other options were offered, too.

Renault 4CV Grand Luxe, 1950. Never offered in the UK, this was Renault's first effort to widen the market for its best seller. The 760cc engine was tuned to produce 21bhp (against 17) and internally there were improvements, such as two interior lights, upholstered inner wheel arches and better seats as well as the normal de luxe fittings. External changes included chromed windscreen-wiper arms, chromed front boot hinges, whitewall tyres, a fog lamp and twin horns, aluminium beading along the rear wing-to-body joints, chromed air-intake embellishers, special polished aluminium front number-plate surround and front boot central trim, chromed body sill trims, lockable engine cover and much else.

Renault 4CV, 1951. In October 1950, the 760cc R-1060 Renault 4CV became the 747cc Renault R-1062, retaining the six-bar plus moustache front, until the three bars succeeded for the 1954 model year. The Renault 750 (as it was designated in the UK) was assembled at Acton from 1949 onwards, with a considerable local content (tyres, dashboard centre section complete with Smiths instruments, electrics, bumpers, etc.), for the British Empire, and a few came on to the home market. The photograph shows three early models at the Renault Owners' Club's 1953 Whitley Wood (Surrey) meeting.

Renault Colorale Prairie, 1951. Having won a major slice of the French small car market with the 4CV, Renault did not ignore the sales opportunities available for larger vehicles. One answer had a 2.4-litre, side-valve '85' (engine bore in mms) at first and, from 1952, the ohv Frégate engine; it sold slowly until 1957, when it disappeared from the sales catalogue after a production run of about 28,000. It found buyers mainly in commercial or rural France and in the francophone colonies with poor road surfaces, but its dumpiness did it no favours in the aesthetics stakes.

Earl's Court Motor Show, 1951. At that year's London venue, Renault exhibited a wide range of 'Seven Fifties', together with the Renault Colorale Prairie MPV, on the right. The model in the foreground is unusual in that it was an Acton-assembled vehicle with round profile bumpers, but it was fitted with a fabric roll-top roof, which was certainly non-standard. At the time, the 4CV Convertible (*décapotable*), of which only sixteen right-hand-drive – all French-built – were ever sold into the British market, had a full soft top, folding down bustle-like to the normal rear window line.

Renault Frégate, 1952. The French actress, Viviane Romance, used this very car to publicize Renault's newly arrived R-1100 family car, sporting non-standard *pneus flancs blancs* (whitewall tyres), seen here cruising around the Arc de Triomphe in a very atmospheric springtime publicity shot. Note the lack of midday (short shadows) traffic, the pre-war Peugeot taxi and Simca Huit *commerciale*, as well as a large white pre-war sports car (left back) close to the famous monument, which could do with a clean-up. One of Sonora Radio's Renault Juva vans hides behind its larger sister.

Renault 4CV, 1952. This is one of the 'hot' 4CVs, the R-1063, with the cutaway front wings (to improve brake cooling), cutaway rear wings (to save weight) and changed lamps (for high power Marchal units) and extra (Marchal) driving lights. This model won its class at Le Mans (1951) and in the Mille Miglia, Alpine Rally and Liège–Rome–Liège the following year. It retained the 747cc capacity, but was tuned to produce 32bhp at 5200rpm; it had a five-speed Pons-Rédélé-Claude gearbox, double shockers at the rear and could top 90mph. Seventy were factory built cars and an unknown number of other conversions were built-up from SAPRAR-supplied kits.

Renault 4CV Hino, 1955. Hino Diesel, now part of Toyota and still manufacturing trucks, took out a licence to assemble the 4CV from 1953 onwards from French CKD (completely knocked down) right-hand-drive kits, with special Japanese-manufactured luxury interiors, lengthened bumper-irons with covers (to meet Japanese car length rules), front grille-mounted winkers, special rear lights, external petrol filler (on the right) and a larger rear window. In 1957, Hino broke the agreement unilaterally, producing their own exact copies until 1963, totalling about 50,000 in all. Almost extinct now, this one was exhibited at the fiftieth Anniversary of the 4CV celebrations in May 1997 at Aubevoye, Renault's test track.

Renault 4CV De Luxe Saloon, 1954. Many discriminating motorists chose Renault's little '*motte de beurre*', 'pat of butter' (this referred to the colour of the paintwork and was the only shade available at the time), for its economy, its comfort and its roadholding over indifferent surfaces. Among these was Jimmy Wilde, ex-world flyweight boxing champion, seen here taking delivery of his new car from Frank Jenkinson, director of Glanfield Lawrence Ltd of Cardiff, then a Renault agent. This R-1062 appears to be a three-bar 1954 Acton-built de luxe model, the Britishness deduced from the round section bumper and semaphore signal in the rear quarter panel and the superior version from the metal sun roof and lever adjustment for the driver's seat position.

Renault Type 4157, 1955. When Pierre Dreyfus took over the fortunes of Renault upon the unexpected death of its first *President Directeur Générale*, Pierre Lefaucheux, one of his first tasks was to finalize the Renault/Latil/SOMUA amalgamation into SAVIEM, Renault's commercial vehicle division. This lorry, to become the Type 4153 in 1956, was a 15-tonner with a six-cylinder, direct-injection, inclined diesel which produced 100bhp up to 1953, but 120bhp later, and was the first fruits of this amalgamation. The vehicle had a powerful compactness about it and was a rugged and enduring performer.

Renault 4CV Sport, 1955. This production line at Billancourt seems light years away from that of the Juvaquatre in 1947. For this one model year, after the diamond Renault badge (*losange*, lozenge) had replaced the round one (*macaron*, macaroon) permanently, a second chromed horn replaced the fog lamp on the front bumper. By this time, the R-1062 had been perfected and this version is often felt to be the best. The only major changes up to its demise in 1961 were the cowled instrument panel ahead of the driver (1956) and the (ex-Dauphine) plate wheels (1958).

Renault 750, 1955. Definitely English models, the one with rounded bumpers and the other with a sterling brother. Pat Moss, no mean motorsport competitor herself and sister of the famous Stirling Moss, often a Renault owner himself, inspects the business end of Renault's little marvel. One can just discern the two round Smiths' dials integrated via two aluminium jointing strips into the centre of a standard dashboard on Acton-built R-1062s. Non-standard are the rear screen diamond and the 'Do not empty' tag on the inside of the engine cover. Pat has been married now for many years to Eric Carlsson, legendary Swedish rally hero.

Renault 'Etoile Filante' Gas Turbine World Record Holder, 1956. Designed by Albert Lory (remembered for the famous Delage 1.5-litre) and driven by Jean Hébert, an inspector for the Département des Mines, the beautifully streamlined 'Shooting Star' 270CV (at 28000rpm) Turbomeca-powered car became (and remains) the world's fastest gas turbine car when it reached 309kph (192mph) at the Salt Lake on 5 September 1956. The excellent publicity generated by this still extant vehicle helped to raise Renault's profile enormously in the USA, just as the Dauphine was about to be launched on to that market.

Renault Dauphine, 1957. Here is one of the very first R-1090 Dauphines and, because of the star-type wheels, its kinship to the 4CV is clear. In the rear compartment, the engine looked very similar, but there was more elbow room around it; in the front compartment, there was more space (despite the battery) and no spare wheel, because it was stowed below in a separate cage, accessed by a drop-down door which bore the number plate; inside there was more leg room, more shoulder room and less austere seats as well as a built-in heater/demister. Truly, a grown-up 4CV.

Renault Dauphine, 1957. Queen Elizabeth II accepted the gift of an R-1090 Dauphine (assembled at Acton) when she visited Flins. Specially finished in powder blue with chromed wire-wheels, the car graced the Royal Mews for years. Later, it passed through the hands of Gordon Offord (Offords of South Kensington were coachmakers to the Royal family for generations and, at that time, London distributors for Renault, and also helped to found the Renault Owners' Club in 1953), W. 'Pop' Challice (a long-time Renault dealer) and various others. 362 GLM was eventually irremediably rolled and scrapped.

Renault Frégate Domaine Station Wagon, 1957. In 1956, the R-1101 version of Renault's large car appeared, based on the earlier 2-litre with its three-bar chrome grille. The growth in Renault's UK sales, thanks to the Dauphine, caused two such vehicles, painted in dark red with gold lettering on a black background, to be added to their fleet. With a special bonnet mascot, outside mirrors, twin Marchal foglamps and a radio, these rare vehicles were on stand-by at Renault's Acton HQ with after-sales staff as a backup to solve in-service problems. Larger tyres and an uprated gearbox were fitted.

Renault Gordini-Dauphine, 1958. Amédée Gordini persuaded the 30bhp 'Ventoux' unit to produce considerably more power without any engine capacity increase by redesigning the inlet manifold to use a 32 mm carburettor (instead of a 28 mm one) and a four-branch exhaust, using the standard silencer. These complemented his redesigned cylinder head, which had inclined valves and a higher lift from the standard camshaft through changing the rocker layout; the new twin water take-off dissipated the extra power's heat and the cast alloy 'G'-initialled rocker box cover reduced tappet noise. Additionally, four speeds inserted into the standard three-speed gearbox casing was a master stroke.

Renault Gordini-Dauphine, 1958. As his own racing car company foundered, Amédée Gordini contracted with Renault to produce a performance version of the Dauphine: the R-1091. The Dauphine-Gordini badges (on the rear engine cover and the front wings) promised a 25 per cent engine power increase through the *sorcellerie* (magic) practised by the engine wizard which, coupled with a fourth speed inveigled into the standard gearbox casing, transformed the vehicle into a little hot shot for its day. Stirling Moss is seen here participating in the 1958 London (Marble Arch)–Paris (Arc de Triomphe) Race, which was front-page news for weeks and created marvellous publicity for Renault.

Renault 4CV Saloon, 1959. The general shape of this little car, which put France back on wheels after the Second World War, changed little over the years. The major external alterations were the six front grille bars giving way to three for the 1954 model and the replacement of the 'star' road wheels for the plate wheels four years later, when the same changes were made to the Dauphine. Other unseen Dauphine-standardized modifications were quietly taken up on a cost-saving basis for the 4CV (such as pressed steel wishbones, wheel hub caps, etc.) and the R-1062 sold strongly until its demise in 1961, when its production lines were replaced with those for another classic-to-be, the Four.

Renault Dauphine, 1959. Although the external shape of this beautiful car remained unchanged throughout its entire production career, the sophisticated North American market required larger diameter sealed beam headlights, special bumper arrangements and particular road wheels to be fitted, these latter replacing the early models' rim-fixing 'star' type, inherited from the 4CV and always being fitted to the American-bound models. The plate wheels (later slotted) became standard worldwide in 1958 and US models of the R-1090 were always fitted as standard with the peppiest versions of the normal engine to increase their everyday performance.

Renault Dauphine, 1959. In its day, this little family saloon was a formidable rally competitor, even if some drivers managed to mismanage it on to its roof. It is interesting that this R-1090 has the older 'star' wheels and, as far as one can see, very little preparation has been undertaken – just a couple of extra lamps on the front. Seen here competing successfully in the 1959 Liège–Rome–Liège Rally, a competitor climbs one of the unbelievably sinuous and badly surfaced Alpine passes; Dauphines finished first and second in class and second and third overall.

Renault Frégate, 1959. Time was running out for the Frégate, seen here in its R-1103 final version, with its triangula badge and oval grille which went with the internal changes of ivory coloured steering wheel and dashboard and ne Dunlopillo seating. It looked like a *passé* American and sold only 6,000-odd examples in this year, but it was still int record-breaking: the Algiers to Cape of Good Hope 14,000 km dash took nine days and eighteen minutes, beating th 1953 Delahaye 135's marker. But the writing was on the wall.

CHAPTER SEVEN

NEW HORIZONS

Ile de Séguin, 1960s. Louis' original workshop is still preserved among the block of trees behind the modern white buildings on the right. When he built his first car there, Seguin Island was a rustic wilderness which, over the years, he bought up, plot by plot, covering it completely with buildings. This floating ship of an island is tethered by its own bridges to Billancourt on the right and to Meudon on the left. Decommissioned now, calmly it awaits redevelopment, possibly as a complex which will house Renault's outstanding heritage.

INTRODUCTION

During the 1960s, the successful Dauphine was joined by the handsome and sporting Floride and a grown-up sibling, the Renault Eight and its Renault Ten derivative and their coupé sisters, as well as by a range of other cars. The Dauphine and its Gordini version were deluxified for a short period with Ondine models and later improved throughout the decade with disc brakes, tougher gearboxes, better rustproofing, 'Aerostable' suspension modifications, etc. First, they were joined by the 2 + 2 derivative, the Floride, with bodywork designed by Ghia, but – because of Ghia's links with Volkswagen with their Karmann-Ghia models – executed by Frua. Dreyfus had realized the dangers of the mono-model culture (later the Beetle would almost scupper Volkswagen) and, ever mindful of the looming Dauphine oversupply to the USA, he accelerated the introduction of the company's newer developments.

This was the first of the all-at-the-front Renault family, made commercially viable as the car market developed out of the immediate penurious necessities of the post-war era and this allowed Renault to break out of the economy car field, to which it had been confined for the most part by those same conditions, and thus to cater to the vast majority of the overall passenger vehicle market potential. A first signpost was the 1958 introduction of a small, forward-control commercial, the Estafette, powered by the Dauphine's 845cc 'Ventoux' engine and four-speed box driving backwards to the front wheels, which leapt quickly to the top of its market segment.

Production of the trusty 4CV, which had steadfastly refused to die, despite the popularity of the Dauphine, was stopped on 6 July 1961 after selling over a million. This allowed production line changes in preparation for the introduction of the revolutionary (for Renault) all-at-the-front, go-anywhere Renault Four, which was to have an even more illustrious career, finally being forced out of production over thirty years later, primarily because of subsequent Euro legislation. The Four had a Dauphine-based engine, preceded by a three-speed gearbox, controlled by a dashboard-mounted gear lever; it also had no-lube, torsion bar suspension, sealed coolant circuit (a first on a small car) and a huge load area, easily accessed by a lift-up, one-piece tailgate. It had no sporting pretensions and long-travel suspension gave it a superb ride, which smothered even major road irregularities, in consequence of which it rolled alarmingly in tight corners but never toppled over. One either loved or loathed the farm-barn, two-box shape and it sold like hot cakes, because it was such excellent value for money.

No sooner had this vehicle appeared than the spiritual successor to the Dauphine, which continued to soldier on until 1968, was launched – the Renault Eight (all-at-the-back), fitted with the Renault's new five-bearing 956cc 'Sierra' engine, followed by the 2 + 2 derivative, the Floride S, which grew up into the Caravelle (with an 1108cc version of the same engine) in 1964. Within three years, Renault had produced a long-nosed version of the Eight, the Ten, and, to cover the market ever more thoroughly, it launched its second trend-setter of the decade, the Renault Sixteen.

With a completely new, all-alloy engine sitting behind the gearbox (as with the Four) and driving the front wheels, the all-torsion bar suspension, sealed coolant system, superbly comfortable seats and sloping hatchback body set new family sized car concepts and standards; even the column-mounted gear change was good, but the awkwardly placed, umbrella-handled handbrake and the idiosyncratic instrumentation were contentious. Renault had another million best-seller on its hands.

Other manufacturers had taken up Renault's original idea of a sporting version of their current family saloon (the 4CV had spawned its sporting look-alike, the R-1063 and the Dauphine-Gordini had its R-1093 'Rallye' Dauphine version). Renault, drawing on Gordini's wizardry, brought out their Eight Gordini 1100 (in 1964), a 1108cc, four-door, 100mph family saloon, which comfortably saw off any class opposition, but it was upstaged in 1966 by a 1255cc version with five-speed gearbox, four-headlight front panel, all-round disc brakes and double shockers at the rear, which sped into 2-litre territory with a top speed of 110mph. The Eight Gordini was every young Frenchman's dream of motorsport training and the famous Coupe Gordini catered for such drivers all over the country from 1965 to '70, encouraging talented drivers to aim for the highest places in all motorsport disciplines.

At the end of the decade, Renault introduced an up-market version of the Four, the Six, which used the same basics, on which there sat a smoother (but nevertheless utilitarian) body, with a more civilized interior, better seats, redesigned dashboard, carpets, door trims, etc. There seemed to be little room in the market place for such a car, but it sold nearly 2 million (it was very popular in Spain) during its eleven-year production run.

There were other shots in Renault's locker – efforts in the commercial field increased their market share. Renault tractors and other horticultural and agricultural equipment were more widely sold and development work with buses, coaches and the Paris Métro and suburban lines brought increased railroad business.

Dreyfus, like Lefaucheux before him, had seen the coming of the European Union and had made plans both with other organizations and alone in order to increase manufacturing capacity into other newly internalized, as well as export, markets. Besides up-dating Billancourt, Renault built new factories at Sandouville (for the Renault Sixteen), at Cléon (gearboxes and engine assembly with some parts supplied from another new factory at Orléans) and expanded existing facilities at Le Mans and Flins.

And it was during this decade that Renault and Gordini started to work more closely with Jean Rédélé of Alpine and with René Bonnet's eponymous firm, until Matra took over.

Renault Frégate Manoir, 1960. This six/eight-seater R-1109 sister to Renault's large saloon widened the model's sales appeal and was aimed squarely at the Safari versions of Citroën's contemporary ID/DS range. It shared the beefier 2141cc 'Etendard' engine with the Domaine (standard estate) and with the Amiral and Grand Pavois saloons, but production was small during its two-year (1959/1960) lifespan. Its closest competitor was the Simca Marly and its advantages were its semi-automatic 'Transfluide' transmission and interior trim identical to the saloon's, but even these blandishments did not make the vehicle any more exportable.

Renault 4CV Beach Buggy, 1960. Ghia was commissioned to customize a batch of fifty late cars in the manner of his Fiat Jolly cars. The windscreen glass stood proud of the A-posts, to which the 'surrey' canopy was attached, the tubular bumpers were specific to type and the headlights were oversize (to meet US vehicle regulations), but the dashboard, engine, transmission, brakes and wheels were standard, even if the wheel hub caps were a little unusual. The plastic cord, which was woven to form the seats, was a weak point and occupants could be disconcerted by the lack of doors. Very few examples have survived.

Renault Ondine Gordini, 1961. In 1961, this de luxe version (R-1090A) of both the Dauphine and the Gordini became available, the former with the 30bhp and the latter with the 40bhp 'Ventoux' engine. Easily distinguished externally from the ordinary versions, they had slotted wheels with whitewall tyres, front and back screen stainless-steel surrounds and gutter trims as well as waist and lower body embellishers, long chromed rear bonnet hinges, special Van Cleef & Arpels-designed badging, a lower front-bumper bar and rubber-faced rear-bumper overriders. Internally, the black dashboard and two-tone steering wheel were allied to two-tone upholstery with four position, reclining front seats and pleated door pockets.

Renault 4L, 1961. This vehicle, the realization of Pierre Dreyfus' 'Blue Jeans' brief for a car to take anyone anywhere, replaced the legendary Renault 4CV and converted the company's all-at-the-back passenger car philosophy to an all-at-the-front one. This ground-breaking R-1120 offered the unprecedented combination of no chassis greasing, sealed coolant system, amazing travel suspension, exceptional economy of operation and more interior space than any other contemporary vehicle of similar overall dimensions. During its long life, it encompassed many special editions (including 4 x 4) and was used by utilities and armed forces.

Renault Rambler, 1961. Renault's 'affair' with AMC (American Motors Corporation) was not an 1980s' phenomenon, for RNUR's Belgian plant in Haren commenced assembly of Rambler CKD (completely knocked down) kits in 1961. But the project was economically unviable and dragged out painfully over five or more years, during which fewer than 5,000 vehicles were manufactured (the kits were often incomplete and spare parts sourcing was a nightmare) and Renault lost a considerable amount of money. After the Dauphine experience in the New World, this was another unfortunate American dream which did nothing to solve the Frégate's succession.

Renault Floride, 1961. To increase Renault's American sales, Pierre Dreyfus commissioned a Dauphine-based sports car from Luigi Segre of Ghia, but, owing to that firm's contractual commitments to Volkswagen and, indirectly, to Karmann, the prototype car was built to Ghia's design by Frua. After a complicated development, Renault presented Ghia's Dauphine GT as the R-1092 Floride at the 1958 Paris Salon; the chassis, with Dauphine mechanicals, was united with bodywork from Chausson in the Brissonneau et Lotz factory (alongside railway equipment!) and this coupé is a late example, the Renault Eight-based Floride S appearing in the following year.

Renault Panoramic Railcar, 1961. Yet another little sideline for France's state-owned vehicle giant was this train, built in their Choisy-le-Roi plant for the SNCF (French Railways) as a city-to-city passenger conveyance, which could carry up to eighty-eight passengers at speeds of up to 130kph. Of particular interest is the upper deck viewing facility. By this time, Renault had also produced the world's first operational gas-turbine locomotive (1952) and was a major rolling-stock manufacturer for the Paris Métro, fitting their carriages with rubber tyres to reduce noise levels.

Renault Floride S, 1962. With the introduction of the 'Sierra'-engined Renault Eight in 1962, Renault was able to update the elegant Dauphine-based Floride with the new car's underpinnings, so the R-1131 Floride S looked like a grown-up Floride, except that the side-located air intakes were smoothed away because the engine drew its cooling air in through the slots on the rear engine cover. The model seen here is a convertible with the hard top in place and powered by the 956cc engine, which would give way to the 1108cc version of the Caravelle in 1964.

Renault 8 Saloon, 1963. Renaults with aluminium cylinder heads and concomitant high combustion-chamber temperatures were always economical, an important sales point. Using a newly introduced, standard R-1132 Renault Eight, seen here at the trial's start, the A.V. Roe Motor Club of Woodford, Cheshire, organized a 24-hour economy run at the end of March 1963. A standard car, driven by a team of amateur drivers with an observer, each drove two 34-mile laps to average 30mph before changing over (observers changed every four laps) and the car covered 720 miles averaging over 51mpg.

Renault 4 Sinpar 4 x 4, 1964. This is a Series One vehicle with small grille (note '4 x 4' logo) and tubular front bumpers, based on an army prototype version of the van, having a de-mountable windscreen, special bonnet supports for the folded windscreen frame, welded-up door frames to add strength, yet having access cutaways, no rear seats and a canvas hood. Are those special extra lights low at the front? This vehicle was participating in the 1964 Rallye des Cimes, where such hybrid vehicles finished first, second and third in the (up to 1000cc) class and fifth overall.

Renault Caravelle, 1964. This car was to the Renault Eight what the Floride had been to the Dauphine – each using their respective saloon's underpinnings, engines and transmissions. The R-1133 Caravelle clearly inherited the Floride's countersunk headlamps and, with the rear engine's radiator relocated to the rear of the bodywork, the Floride's lateral air intakes ahead of the rear wheels were modified to leave only hints of their past. Born in 1962, the model used the tough 'Sierra' five-main-bearing engine and was available as a convertible or a fixed-head coupé. The last one was manufactured in 1968.

Renault 8 Gordini 1100, 1964. Having appreciably improved the Dauphine's 'Ventoux' engine within strict cost parameters, Amédée Gordini next 'tweaked' Renault's new 'Sierra' engine. This R-1134 four-door, well-equipped, comfortable, sporting wolf-in-sheep's clothing could top the ton, yet was capable of transporting four adults and their luggage quite economically. The upgrade's essentials were two Solex twin-choke carburettors, a reworked camshaft, a cross-flow hemispherical head with twin spark passages and a four-branch, free-flow exhaust manifold and this formula, '*bolide bleu à bandes blanches*' (blue fireball with white stripes), as a contemporary song put it, led to a significant French resurgence in international motorsport.

Renault 4 Parisienne, 1966. In December 1963, Renault introduced an *haute couture* variation of the R-1123 for their 1964 range, for those who wanted the *cachet* of the *chic* (style) Four, which was selling very well, but who wanted to be a little different from the common herd. In fact, it was a black export model with stuck-on yellow canework, as seen, or, alternatively, available with either a green or a red tartan pattern. For 1965, there was a cloth interior and, for 1966, Renault offered a second colour, blue, still with the same appliqués. The Parisienne disappeared from the Four range in 1969.

Car of the Year, 1966. Pierre Dreyfus (left), then current head of the RNUR, receives this prestigious award, organized by the Dutch *Auto Visie* magazine and judged by a panel of international motoring correspondents, for the innovative R-1150 Renault 16. The French company has been a formidable competitor for this trophy over the years, winning four times (Renault 16 in 1966, Renault 9 in 1982, Renault Clio in 1991 and Renault Mégane in 1997), being runner up three times (Renault 15/17 in 1972, Renault 5 in 1973 and Renault 25 in 1985) and bronze medallist twice (Renault 12 in 1970 and Renault 30 in 1976).

Renault 8 Gordini 1100, 1966. Long-distance racing has always had a large following throughout continental Europe, initially with the early city-to-city races, in which Renault shone, and later with the Mille Miglia, Le Mans 24 Hour Race and others. The Spa Francorchamps 24 Hour Race for 'production' cars was the venue for a Renault team victory in the *Coupe du Roi* (King's Cup), the team seen here in close formation. Note that these are R-1134 versions with extra lights in the front panel (except for last car) and a couple more for good measure.

Renault 16 GL, 1967. At its 1965 launch, the R-1150 breached virgin market territory – a mid-sized, quiet, comfortable, family car with foldable rear seats and a huge, windowed opening at the back, useful for loading something really bulky, if needs be. It heeled over unusually in corners on its long-travel, torsion-bar suspension, but it coped brilliantly with European – and even worse – roads. Immediately, other manufacturers scuttled away to design their interpretations. Here is a relatively early example, retaining the purity of its innovative lines, uncluttered by trim, yet showing an interesting design touch in the patterned wheel hub caps.

Renault 8 Gordini 1300, 1967. Amédée Gordini's cross-flow cylinder head changed Renault's 956cc 'Sierra' engine (42bhp) into a 1108cc fire-breather (95bhp). The ultimate R-1135 standard model illustrated had a 1255cc version (110bhp) and a five-speed gearbox, all-round disc brakes, a comprehensive dashboard and comfortable seats, making this a genuine GT saloon with an 110mph top speed (with the 'long' 9 x 34 final drive), unequalled by any contemporary class contender. The Coupe Gordini, fashioned around the model, nurtured a whole generation of French motorsport fanatics, many later being well known in the top echelon of automotive competition.

Renault 8 Gordini 1300, 1967. Gordini's original tuning 'tweaks' to the five-main-bearing 'Sierra' engine had proved that the unit was rugged and could be driven hard. The 1255cc engine (1269cc in Group Two form) was a development of the earlier 1108cc version and, coupled with a five-speed gearbox, based on the earlier four-speeder, and four searchlights on the front made this a formidable war horse, with which many national rally and autocross championships were won before the advent of rally specials. Here, Piot and Roure, the outright winners of the 1967 Rallye dei Fiori (Rally of the Flowers), hurry over the Caccia Pass.

Renault 8, 1968. When the Dauphine grew up, it became the R-1130 8 in 1962, although they sold alongside each other for six years. Boxy, yet surprisingly aerodynamic (aided by the indented-V bonnet), it offered all-round disc brakes (a first in class), a new, smooth, five-main-bearing, ohv engine, with sealed coolant system (inherited from the 4), exceptional seating comfort (universally extolled in the motoring press), remarkable economy and a competitive price ticket. During a ten-year production run, it was manufactured in South America, France, Spain, Bulgaria (as Bulgarenault) and assembled all over the world to the tune of over 1½ million. A special Renault 8 'Alconi' sports version was manufactured in South Africa.

Renault 4 'Plein Air', 1968. Between May 1968 and April 1970, Sinpar converted for Renault a small number of R-1123 Fours as recreational vehicles, some of which were 4 x 4s. This 'Open Air' had standard mechanicals, de luxe seating, controls and dashboard and little body strengthening was necessary, owing to the Four's tough punt floor. The rear tailgate was halved horizontally and flapped down and two thin chains were meant to keep the crew aboard! A handful of genuine right-hand-drive examples came to the UK and two exist, although a further few DIY copies were also created.

Renault 16TS, 1969. Martin Lumby hurries his R-1151 towing a Bluebird Europe 1 caravan through one of the circuit tests at Mallory Park during the fifteenth British Caravan Road Rally, organized by the Caravan Club from 18–20 April 1969. There were over 120 contestants and the event contained a 230-mile night-navigation rally, six circuit tests and a concours, with the Renault team emerging ahead of everyone else. The Sixteen's good spread of torque, well-stepped gearing and comfort stood the Cambridge entrants in good stead. The wheel hub caps have been removed in the interests of safety.

Renault 8S Saloon, 1969. Some customers wanted an Eight Gordini lookalike costing significantly less, being cheaper to insure and yet remaining sporty. At the 1968 Paris Salon, Renault introduced the R-1136 Eight S, available initially in bright yellow only, which was just over half as expensive and still had the four-light front panel. (The centre ones were not halogens.) The 1,108cc, 60bhp 'Sierra' engine and four-speed gearbox came from the recently defunct Caravelle, the dashboard sported all the meaningful dials and there were lightweight seats with patterned facings. The car sold in limited numbers during its two-year production life.

CHAPTER EIGHT

ALL CHANGE

Renault 5, 1970. If any car typifies the direction which the design of small family cars took in the 1970s, then this, the first of the superminis, must be it. This is the TL version of the first series (slotted wheels and adjustable back rest on the front seats), with the striped dashboard and pushmepulyu, dash-piercing gear lever, scissor strut for the hatch and non-opening rear windows. It was the first car in its class to have plastic bumpers and the long-travel torsion-bar suspension made for a very comfortable ride.

INTRODUCTION

The Renault Four soldiered on throughout the 1970s, having undergone a major revamp in 1967 (new bonnet with headlights incorporated in the grille and a four-speed gearbox and updated dashboard), which widened its loyal following. Replying to Citroën's 2CV-based Méhari, Renault started selling a plastic-bodied 'Rodéo Four', based on the Four and made by ACL, part of the Teilhol Group, which was joined by a 'Rodéo Six' (still Four-based) version in 1973 (both being available in four body styles). The pair sold steadily throughout the decade into the rural market, as they could be hosed clean, inside and out.

The Eight Gordini 1300 disappeared in 1970 at the 'Jour G', the ordinary Eight soldiering on until 1973, although latterly manufactured only in FASA's Spanish plant. The Ten lasted until 1971. Meanwhile, the 1970 Paris Show saw the European launch of the new 'all-at-the-front' Renault Twelve, which had developed unusually. The design was initiated by Renault in 1965, primarily for Willys do Brasil, Renault's partner in that country. It was about to be launched there when Ford bought up the São company and the car, slightly modified, was launched on that market as the Ford Corcel. Together with the estate, the Gordini version was launched within a year, the latter primarily to replace the Eight Gordini in the Coupe Gordini. A 'warm' TS version and an automatic (TR) version also joined the range before an update (new front and back) in 1976.

Renault returned to the 2 + 2 field with two coupés based on the Twelve; the Fifteen had the Twelve's engine and the Seventeen had the Sixteen's all-alloy unit, but, from the side, they looked quite dissimilar, owing to clever differences in glass area.

Renault's 1970s' blockbuster was the Renault Five, a COTY winner and first of the superminis. To keep costs down, the retained 'Ventoux' and 'Sierra' engines were mounted longitudinally at the front, behind the gearbox, with torsion-bar suspension giving the car a smooth, if roly-poly, ride. A warm TS model (with Renault Twelve TS engine) was introduced in 1975 and an Alpine (Gordini) version appeared in 1978, an early pocket rocket with a cross-flow cylinder head, five-speed gearbox, special wheels, deep front spoiler and 110mph top speed capability. The company had yet another million seller on their hands.

Apart from connections with MAN and Alfa Romeo, who sold SAVIEM heavy vehicles, Renault had links with Volvo, DAF and HD, sold engines to DAF and Lotus and outboard motors to Mercury. The Spanish FASA factory was producing over 130,000 vehicles a year and Renault had a significant presence throughout South America, Romania, Turkey and Yugoslavia.

The 1973 Yom Kippur War and the oil crisis sent shock waves throughout the western world. Nevertheless, Renault withstood them better than most others in the vehicle manufacturing industry, by flexibility of production plants' programmes and by diversifications, resulting in Renault owning Couache, later Renault-Marine, and Moteurs Bernard, a lawn-mower manufacturer, later Renault-Leisure.

Way back in 1966, after secret negotiations, Peugeot and Renault had agreed to co-operate, which resulted in the Douvrin engine factory, the Ruitz transmission systems complex and the modernization of both the Chausson and the Brissonneau et Lotz bodyworks. Peugeot's volte-face in 1974 to amalgamate with ailing Citroën shocked Renault, but it bounced back by eventually gaining control of and incorporating the long-established Berliet commercial vehicle manufacturing company within the SAVIEM family, thus forming France's largest such grouping. Shared patent deposition ceased. Renault bought Micmo, the Gitane bicycle manufacturer, not to mention buying Vélosolex, which gave Peugeot's mopeds a hard time.

Ironically, Renault's Fourteen, introduced in 1977, was powered by a Douvrin-manufactured 1218cc transverse engine with gearbox in the sump (à la Mini), also to be found in Peugeot's 104. In size, the five-door hatchback fitted conveniently between the Twelve and the Sixteen and was comfortable, economical and refined, but it was too bland and bulbous to be very popular and was prone to serious rust.

Social unrest influenced Renault's plans – the costly strikes in 1971 and 1973 were overshadowed by a nine-weeks' strike in 1975. Renault lost 100,000 vehicles' production and went into the red and the launch of the Fourteeen was delayed for six months and that of the Eighteen for over a year.

The Renault Eighteen answered Ford's Cortina and GM's Cavalier/Ascona. A front-wheel-drive, three-box saloon, joined by an estate and, in the next decade, a 2 + 2 coupé, it was a 'Eurobland', with two petrol engine choices and a diesel, and based on the ageing Twelve.

In 1975, Renault returned to the large car market with the Renault Twenty and Thirty, both sharing the same five-door, hatchback bodyshell (unusual in this market class), but with different engines, a new 2-litre, in-line, ohc four in the Twenty and the new Douvrin-built V6 for the Thirty. Later, the Twenty became Renault's first diesel passenger car and, combined with the Thirty, over ¾ of a million were manufactured over nine years.

It was during this decade that Renault slowly took over Alpine, European 2-litre prototype champions and Monte-Carlo Rally winners in 1971 and 1973, the year that they were world rally champions. In 1977, to gain publicity, Renault entered Formula One, challenging Ford's V8 engine supremacy with a controversial 1.5-litre, turbocharged unit. Forced induction was to be the keynote of Renault's marketing throughout the 1980s, as evinced by the prototype of the turbocharged, mid-engined Renault Five Turbo, first exhibited at the 1978 Paris Salon.

Another big shock for Renault came in 1978, when Peugeot took over all Chrysler's European operations, which Dreyfus had declined in 1974, and pushed Renault into No. 2 spot in France.

The 1980s were to be a tempestuous time for *la Régie*.

Renault 6, 1970. In 1968, with this essentially grown-up Renault Four, *la Régie* sought to introduce a market gap-filler below the Renault Sixteen. The visibly less boxy Six was more civilized, in that it offered Renault Eight quality seats, a less quirky dashboard and an effective fresh-air, heating and demisting system, combined with more sound insulation and a less spartan finish. In an effort to broaden its appeal, a TL version was introduced in 1970, sales of which then overshadowed this basic version. The Six did not have the cheeky appeal of her more basic sister and, although more than 1½ million had been sold, it disappeared in 1979.

Renault 10, 1970. This saloon was a Renault Eight with a nose and tail job ! The longer front considerably increased the front boot luggage capacity and the stretched tail assisted aerodynamics, while the extra weight smoothed the Eight's nervous ride. 'Sierra' engined, one and all, and known variously as Ten, Elevenhundred, Major or Ten-Thirteenhundred, the first (1108cc) R-1190 version had round headlights with wraparound frontwinker-cum-sidelight cluster (retained in the USA throughout its life) and a burnished alloy embellisher between the rear lights. Sharing all the Eight's underpinnings and suspension, it was manufactured from 1965 to '72.

Renault 12, 1970. Developed as a world car by Renault in conjunction with Willys do Brasil, it appeared as the original Ford Corcel, because in the meantime Kaiser had sold out to Ford. Renault sold its 8½ per cent share in the company and the production rights to Project 117, the profit being re-invested in IKA, Argentina. With its 1289cc 'Sierra' engine preceding the four-speed gearbox driving the front wheels and a slippery body shape, the R-1170 Twelve offered excellent seats, typically Gallic road-holding, toughness and economy. In almost twenty years, nearly 3 million Renault versions of this under-rated vehicle were manufactured worldwide in Europe, South America and Australia.

Renault 5, 1972. This vehicle, the first of the superminis, was to be at or near the top of the best-seller league tables until it was superseded by the Superfive, thirteen years later. The first versions had a dashboard-mounted, pushmepulyu gear lever and the longitudinally mounted 956cc 'Sierra' engine for the TL version, preceded by a four-speed gearbox, which was lifted straight out of the original Renault Eight. Torsion bars bestowed an absorbent ride on this hatchback and the sheer versatility of the cheeky newcomer ensured an immediate and loyal following. Plastic bumpers were a pioneering novelty.

Renault 6TL, 1972. As Renault sales in the UK climbed, so the Southampton import centre became too small to handle the importing and preparation of all the cars. Accordingly, a second import centre was opened at Goole in Yorkshire. Here, the cars are being PDI'd (pre-delivery inspected) one by one at that new facility and, with over 150,000 vehicles annually coming into the UK in the late 1990s, this period picture seems incredibly antediluvian. The first vehicle is one of the first series 'Sierra'-engined TLs, distinguishable from its lesser sibling by its slotted wheels and additional air intake just above the front bumper.

Renault 12 Gordini, 1973. By now, after all its problems, this R-1173 successor to the inimitable 'Gord' (Renault 8 Gordini) had reached maturity, with the temperature-sensitive cooling fan and the bonnet scoop feeding cool air to the greedy twin Weber carburettors to ensure a regularly delivered standard 125bhp from the Sixteen-derived 1565cc front-mounted engine. Finally available in 1974 with bumpers (the auxiliary lights were standard), tinted windows and high-back seating, it would have been a real 115mph Q-car, but the obligatory special blue with specific-to-model white striping blew it. Only 5,138 genuine examples were made from June 1970 to June '74.

Renault 15 TL, 1973. This first series car is really a Twelve in a party frock, using that R-1170 saloon's floorpan, 1289cc ohv 'Sierra' five-main-bearing engine followed by a four-speed gearbox with floor-change and running gear, all clothed in three-door, two-light coupé bodywork; internal decoration was quirkily Gallic, with large, individual peaks sheltering each round dial on the fascia and with unusual but comfy seats. Produced between 1971 and '79, the R-1300 15 and sister car, the R-1312 17, sold just over 300,000 examples.

Renault 16 TX, 1973. This R-1156 was the luxury version of the world's first large-scale production, medium-sized, five-door hatchback. It boasted an all-alloy, 1.6-litre engine with cross-flow cylinder head, preceded by a five-speed gearbox, operated via an excellent steering column change. Long travel, all-round, torsion bar suspension coupled with sumptuous armchair seats offered superlative travel comfort, while four dashboard-adjustable QI headlamps, disc brakes, rear wash/wipe, sealed coolant system, tinted windows, plenty of electric goodies and a huge boot came as standard. No wonder nearly 2 million 16s found willing buyers during a fifteen-year life cycle.

Renault 5TL, 1973. Another first-on-the-market car for Renault was their 5 supermini, which had a big car ride, comfy seats, roomy boot, plastic bumpers, economy of operation, disturbing roll angles when pushed and pushmepulyu dashboard gearlever. It retained the longitudinally mounted front engine with preceding gearbox layout of the 4, the first power plant being the 845cc 'Ventoux' unit and, later, various sizes of the 'Sierra' unit. Torsion bar suspension all round was a major ride advantage. The TL version seen here had the five-bearing 'Sierra' engine, denoted by the slotted road wheels.

Alpine Renault A-441 2-litre European Sports Championship Winner, 1974. Jean Rédélé had long dreamed of an Alpine win at Le Mans and, with Renault making a partial take-over of Alpine in January 1973, financing became available to develop his 1972 all-enveloping, tail step-spoilered A-440 *barquette* (little boat) with V6 Renault Gordini Type CH1B engine into a winner. Both engine and aerodynamics were continuously improved by the Renault-Gordini engineers at Viry-Châtillon, until it became a championship winner and the basis for the development of the future turbocharged Le Mans winner four years later.

Renault Rodéo, 1975. Renault felt the need to compete in the basic car market, where Citroën's Méhari had done well and Renault's 4 was 'too posh'. ACL built the vehicles, Teilhol marketed them and Renault approved them for sale through their dealership network. All versions used the 4's underpinnings with all-plastic bodywork in various versions (Evasion, Chantier, Quatre Saisons, Coursière, etc.) with different mechanical specifications and sometimes with Sinpar 4 x 4 conversions. The Rodéo 4 had a raised bonnet and round headlamps and the 6 had a flush bonnet with rectangular headlamps. They sold mostly in rural districts or for leisure purposes.

Renault 5TS, 1976. The TS was to the TL as the Cooper was to the Mini. Available only as a three-door hatchback, its peppy 1289cc 'Sierra' engine, coupled to a four-speed gearbox, propelled the R-1224 to well over 90mph. Apart from firmer suspension, the changes were mostly in the cab – 'horse collar', high back, fabric-covered front seats and a rev counter on the dashboard. Externally, there was a stainless-steel embellishing strip along the lower sill but no anti-damage plastic panels. This early model does not have colour-coded bumpers.

Renault 5 Automatic, 1976. No gearchanging hassle made this a great favourite with lady shoppers, who further appreciated its comfortable seats, economy, chic looks, a low-lip hatch for the goodies and folding rear seats for that extra-awkward load. The 1.3-litre engine was fitted to offset transmission power loss and this version always sported the (then) fashionable vinyl roof. A few extra centimetres in the chassis allowed two back doors and the plastic side strakes were another effective Renault novelty, later much copied by other manufacturers. Henceforward, Renault always tried to offer an automatic in their small car range.

Renault 17 TS, 1977. This second series half-sister to the Fifteen continued the distinguishing side windows and louvred rear quarter light feature of this upmarket 2 + 2 coupé and it too utilized the Renault 12's underpinnings, but not its running gear. The tasteful and comfortable interior offered a revised dashboard, while the Renault 16-derived engine and five-speed gearbox and front disc brakes allowed a 100mph-plus top speed. In sales terms, the model sold less than half as well as its sibling, although both were true hatchback coupés whose unusual styling restricted their market appeal.

Renault Estafette Range, 1976. In 1958, the 'Galion' was replaced by the R-2130 'Estafette'; significantly, it was the first series-produced front-wheel-drive in Renault's history – and, although it started life with the Dauphine's three-main-bearing 'Ventoux'engine, it was updated in 1961, as the R-2132, with Renault's new five-main-bearing 'Sierra' engine. After fifteen years of production, the appearance had been updated and the flimsier pieces strengthened, thus making it more reliable and less of a *jolie laide* (maid of all work). It was used by the gendarmerie, the police and the armed forces and formed the basis for a range of motor homes.

Renault 5GTL, 1976. In an astute move, Renault mated their torquey 1300cc 'Sierra' engine to a five-speed gearbox with a high final-drive ratio in the TL and GTL, which allowed well over 60mpg on long runs, coupled with a surprising turn of speed when wound up. It shared the family trait of first-class comfort and, available in three and five-door form, the cheeky shape carried Renault's pioneering anti-damage side panels, made of grey plastic to blend better with similarly coloured plastic bumpers.

Renault 12L Saloon, 1977. Already over five years in production when it received its facelift for the 1976 model year, all versions were unchanged mechanically, but a blander front grille pushed the sidelight/winker cluster down into a new stronger front bumper, which lost its rubber overriders, the air vents on the C-post changed from embellished vertical slots on the panel's leading edge to a plastic-grilled rectangle almost on the waistline and the TL sported fussier wheel hub caps. The rear aspect gained overriderless bumpers, as at the front, but without inset lights, larger one-block lights and a black boot-lip trim.

Renault 18 GTS, 1978. Renault's successful saloon answer to Ford's Cortina and GM's Cavalier/Ascona, this R-1341 was a new and thoroughly modern, mainstream design, having good luggage capacity (even teddy is applauding!), a supple, but not roly-poly, ride and comfortable seating. For the first time, the French manufacturer had a strongly competitive car (range) in the peculiarly British 'repmobile' market, in which low maintenance costs and high residuals played a paramount role. The GTS model offered the option of a fabric sliding roof. The steep rise in Renault's UK sales indicated that the Renault 18 recipe was a good one.

Renault 18 Estate, 1978. This was the R-1351 mid-range (TS) edition of Renault's smart family class load carrier, which was launched simultaneously with the saloon. With the one-piece rear seat tilted forward, the seat back lay flat, thus offering a huge, level floor which, coupled with comfortable front seats (complete with headrests), light controls and quietness, made this a favourite with reps. The long gearing, economical engine and good noise suppression and a supple ride were remarkable in a vehicle of this type at the time. It was manoeuvrable and sold well in country areas, too.

Renault Alpine A-442B V6 Turbo Le Mans winner, 1978. After Matra's successful Le Mans victories (1972 to 1974), Renault sought to keep the French flag flying. The 'toe in the water' effort in 1976 resulted in a blown turbo; all three cars failed in 1977, but, in 1978, Jean-Pierre Jaussaud and Didier Pironi won the race for Renault with the A-442B development, which was fêted down the Champs-Elysées. The engine was a highly developed, turbocharged version of that first used in the 1974 2-litre European championship-winning Alpine A-441 (see p. 110).

Renault 14 TS, 1979. The R-1212 was the only fruit of the finally abortive Renault/Peugeot marriage and its anonymity added little to Renault's reputation. The 1218cc engine, which had first appeared in Peugeot's 104 four years earlier, was Renault's first transverse, front-wheel-drive engine foray; it sported serpentine and unpredictable belts, but the TS version did exceed the ton. The uninspiring, five-door hatch (the only version) was notoriously rust prone and the car disappeared in 1982, mourned by few. It is probably best remembered for its metallic orange 'Safrane' edition and its burgundy 'Regency' version (celebrating the wedding of Prince Charles and Lady Diana Spencer), both models having 'AMIL' alloy road wheels.

Renault 20TS, 1979. Introduced to the UK market in August 1977, the Renault 30 bodyshell was the first of the co-operative partners to be furnished with the Douvrin in-line, ohc, four-cylinder, 110bhp/1995cc engine for the R-1272 20 TS hatchback, which slotted in between the TL version, using the 16-derived, all-alloy engine and the Renault 30TS, which was powered by another PRV-Douvrin co-operative engine, the V6. In 1979 it was upgraded with a five-speed gearbox, thus improving this large yet economical, gadget-laden executive comfortmobile. Large luxury hatchbacks were unusual and the 20 and 30 ranges were both succeeded by another such, the Renault 25 range in 1984.

CHAPTER NINE

THE TURBOCHARGED YEARS

Renault Vesta 2, 1987. While other manufacturers were just talking earnestly about fuel economy and its importance, Renault was doing something about it. Following the fuel crises of the 1970s, the French Industry Minister set a research target of 3-litres/100 km (94.2mpg) for a prototype – at a time when a Renault 5 TL, 1981's most economical car, averaged 47.1mpg! After testing Vesta 1 and Vesta+, Vesta 2 averaged 100.5mpg (72/103/137) and set a world record of 145.6mpg at an average of 62mph on the Bordeaux–Paris autoroute. It had a 716cc, 27bhp, three-cylinder petrol engine and five-speed gearbox.

INTRODUCTION

As Renault moved out of the 1970s with a flurry of activities, including a huge contract with the Soviet Union for welding technology, development of machine tools and a complete assembly line for cylinder-head manufacture, a rationalization of its Mexican factories, a partnership with the Portuguese government for a local automobile industry and a massive boost to make its Spanish FASA subsidiary No. 1 in that country by means of a new factory at Valencia, it looked towards North America in the hope of erasing the Dauphine bad dream. Foreign manufacturers had made huge inroads into the US market and American Motors Corporation, the smallest of Detroit's 'Big Four', was looking to Europe for help with its 'economy' car developments. In a few short weeks, Renault supplanted Peugeot as the provider of such a car – the Renault Five 'Le Car' and the mid-sized Renault Eighteen range – and finalized plans to build the forthcoming Nine in American Motors' Kenosha plant. By 1980, Renault owned nearly half of AMC and was strengthening its Colombian plant (Renault held 70 per cent of that market) and Renault Argentina (who held over 20 per cent of that market). It was also working more closely with Volvo, who now part-owned DAF, a customer for some 80,000 Renault engines per year.

Following Renault's absorption of Berliet into SAVIEM, which transmuted into RVI (Renault Véhicules Industriels), it started to work together with the Mack Company, the second largest manufacturer of over-15-ton lorries in the USA. Renault bought 20 per cent of the American company, which then sold RVI trucks up to 15 ton as 'Midliners' under the bulldog emblem. Renault further bought (ex-Chrysler) Dodge Trucks from Peugeot and, in becoming third largest European commercial vehicle manufacturer, picked up a large network of European outlets.

Having won Le Mans in 1978 and entered Formula One the previous year, the 1980s saw a huge increase in the public's awareness of the French marque as a high-tech company through its success in motorsport. Familiar names were Renault Five Turbo, Renault Eleven Turbo, Renault Twenty-One Turbo, Renault Superfive GT Turbo – all of them winners, let alone the Renault Formula One turbo racer.

The frantic commercial pace set by Renault paid off; it rode out the storms of 1980 while Peugeot suffered, and it regained the leadership of the French market as well as of the European market. Its success, from which its share-owning workers benefited, was helped by the introduction of the ever-economical, five-door Renault Five, the fast-selling, new Fuego range, the new diesel versions of the Twenty and Thirty and a comprehensive range of Master and Trafic commercial vehicles, which quickly became major league players.

The unremarkable, COTY-winning Nine was a robot-produced amalgam of contemporary automotive blandness which lacked Gallic flair, but enabled Renault to deliver an economy car (the Alliance), as had been promised, to their ailing AMC colleagues. Its hatchback sibling, the Eleven (aka Encore and, later, GTA in the USA) took over from the Fourteen and sold strongly until superseded by the Nineteen range at the end of the decade. Meanwhile, the Eighteen range – which had never offered a hatch version – and its coupé sibling, the Fuego, gave way to the Twenty-One series and the Twenty/Thirty range was superseded by the Renault Twenty-Five. These ranges further enhanced the earlier models' pioneering penetration of the fleet/business market, as well as of the luxury sector, since the Douvrin straight-four and V6 power units were refined and made more economical.

The development costs of these engine refinements were shared across the range, the larger unit being fitted to the two new Alpine models (called Renault Five Turbo 1 and 2 and, even later, GTA in the UK), the first all-Renault-developed Alpine since the completion of the Dieppe firm's take-over in 1977. That factory's competition preparation and fibre-glass expertise was utilized additionally in the production of the Renault Five Alpine (Gordini) Turbo and of the Superfive GT Turbo as well as of the Espace.

Almost contemporaneous with the launch of the Twenty-Five range came the introduction of the first modern European people-carrier, the Matra-inspired Renault Espace. Unlike every other marque's anterior claimant to the MPV title, the Espace was never a van; it was purpose designed, with a galvanized steel chassis clothed in plastic panels. Despite Matra and Heuliez' utmost assistance, Renault could never make enough of them and it became an icon, which others have since sought to emulate.

Another mid-decade launch was the Renault Superfive, with a transverse engine replacing the Five's longitudinal unit, smoother bodywork, updated and roomier interior – all guaranteed to ensure another million seller. The turbocharged version, the Superfive GT Turbo was every hooligan's GTI-baiter and passed into supermini lore, while the Monaco version (Baccara in most markets) retained limo-style leather upholstery, alloy wheels and posh paint to court the moneyed set.

At the end of the decade, the conservative Renault Nineteen range was launched; the hatches and saloons were more solid, better finished, quieter and comfier than their predecessors. No wonder it became Germany's No. 1 imported car and needed a winner like Laguna to succeed it after six years.

And, although it faded from the UK in mid-decade, the irreplaceable Renault Four soldiered steadily on into the 1990s and lasting fame.

Renault had hoped that its Formula One racer would beat the world's best, but, despite its intrinsic brilliance and occasional success, it was a 'committee car' and Renault withdrew in 1984 to rethink its strategy. Five years later, it was back, but only as an engine supplier to the famous Williams GP team and this combination proved a repeated winner in the 1990s. If the 1980s had launched Renault on to an increasing high, the 'American Dream' turned sour and a world recession added to its woes, plunging it deep into the red. In 1984 they lost a record 12½ billion francs and sought government assistance; part of the painful cure was to sell their AMC operation in 1987 to a resurgent Chrysler, who as a financially troubled company had been a recipient of USA government aid not long previously. What an irony!

But Renault had been down before and showed remarkable resilience in coming back yet again to perform amazingly well in the years leading up to its centenary.

Renault 5 Turbo, 1980. Developed from an idea by Jean Terramorsi, whose death from cancer denied him the chance to see his brainchild in production, this two-seater 'Five On Steroids' featured a longitudinal, mid-mounted, alloy headed turbocharged 1370cc engine, producing 185bhp. The original version (1,362 built) featured a space-age, colour coordinated interior, no luggage space, aluminium and plastic body panels, suspension shared with the Renault Alpine A 310/V6 and it offered prodigious performance, yet it was perfectly tractable. Wide haunches required accurate width estimation and high power output coupled with a short wheelbase demanded respect, especially in the wet.

Renault 18 Turbo, 1980. To capitalize on their Formula One turbocharging technology, Renault took an Eighteen GTS, to which they added the 1565cc, crossflow-headed, all-alloy engine from the Renault 16, but fitted with low compression pistons and a turbocharger, alloy road wheels, up-and-over flexible tail spoiler, some side decals shouting 'Turbo', together with an up-spec. interior, and it became the first mass-produced, mid-range, inexpensive, turbocharged saloon. Despite somewhat peaky power delivery, the engine and general demeanour of the R-1345 seduced both road testers and many customers, so raising Renault's sales profile considerably.

Renault Fuego GTX, 1980. With a clear family resemblance to the 18 and a common platform, this was the first series, top model Fuego with a 1995cc, single ohc engine from the Renault 20, alloy road wheels, headlamp wash/wipe, long-range auxiliary lamps and five-speed gearbox, making it many friends in the coupé market. A genuine four-seater (unlike most of its competitors), with high-back front seats and split rear seats to increase load capacity, the heated goldfish-bowl hatch (with wash/wipe facility) presaged the tail of the 11, but the fluted waistline was a unique distinguishing feature which helped to give movement to the car's overall shape.

Renault 7 (Siete) GTL, 1980. Although this is a 1980 car, it had been commercialized for some years by Spain's FASA-Renault through a co-operative development between themselves and Renault (France). The 'three box' vehicle was important for Hispanic markets and the joint venture also helped Renault to offer the five-door hatch option quickly. (Compare this picture with the top image on p. 112.) The Spanish Siete had a unique front (and back) a single-blade bumper with rubber overriders and not the plastic mouldings of the 5; the dashboard was simpler and the five-bearing 'Sierra' engine was always fitted.

Renault 5TX, 1981. Another Renault production 'first' was the 'little limo' idea, offering a refined cloth interior with roll-top headrests for the driver and passenger, split rear seats which folded to provide a large carrying capacity (normally concealed with a cover), a comprehensively equipped dashboard, 'boutique' leather-rimmed steering wheel, tinted glass all round, including electric front windows, rear wash/wipe to clear the outside of the heated hatch window, metallic paintwork with a discreet coachline, 'AMIL' alloy road wheels with radial-ply tyres, power steering (much needed!) and a fashionable and effective aerodynamic front spoiler. All these features were fitted as standard and converted many a 'Sloane Ranger' to the chic Cinq.

Renault 5 Gordini (Alpine) Turbo, 1981. In appearance, this three-door-only, turbocharged version of the 5 hatchback was an amalgam of its new turbo predecessor (deep front spoiler with fog lamps) and the contemporary TX (top of the range fittings and exterior finish) with the addition of new alloy road wheels. Renault capitalized on their turbocharger competition experience to keep the 5 in contention with the improving multi-valve competition, before the advent of the Superfive, so innovation was under the bonnet. Unusually, the turbocharger compressed air into the upstream, pressurized carburettor with the resultant combustible mixture's temperature lowered through an air-to-air intercooler.

enault 18 American, 1983. As Renault opened up the USA market for their cars through their links with the American
Iotor Corporation, the Renault 18 sold in larger numbers. A reverse spin-off prolonged the car's life in European
larkets through this smart special edition based on the TS model, but featuring specific-to-type, alloy road wheels, high-
uality, Bedford cord seat facings, a moulded, boot lip spoiler, black-over-silver paint (only), side rubbing strip and
romed strip, wheelarch eyebrows. The combination proved popular enough to support the launch of an American 2
lition on the British market.

enault 30TX, 1984. Peugeot, Renault and Volvo established a joint engine-manufacturing plant at Douvrin to produce
all-alloy, single ohc, V6 engine, which each could use for their prestige model; hence the Renault 30, first introduced
1977 as the TS, used it throughout its life. The later, more luxurious TX model also had a five-speed gearbox with
uise control, fuel injection, alloy road wheels, central locking, tinted windows with electrically operated sun roof,
adlamp wash/wipe as well as other upmarket refinements and had an automatic gearbox option. Despite a 120mph top
eed, strong class competition restricted sales considerably.

Renault 18 Turbo Mark 2, 1984. As the Mark 2 updates were applied across the 18 range, so the Turbo's grille wa updated (the half mask at the top improved aerodynamics) and cross-spoke alloy road wheels were introduced, althoug some UK examples were fitted with a different pattern, similar to those on the Mark 2 estate cars. Internally, Bedfo cord-faced seats were offered and the engine was uprated to give a 125mph top speed, indecently fast for a medium-size family saloon of that era. The garish 'Turbo' decals remained an acquired taste . . . or not.

Renault 4 GTL, 1985. By the mid-1980s, the inimitable shape had gained (front) disc brakes, Renault 5 wheels and 'smarter' interior as Type 1128. The three-main-bearing, 845cc 'Ventoux' (ex-Dauphine) engine with three-spe gearbox had given best to the five-main-bearing 1108cc 'Sierra' (ex-Renault Eight) engine with four-speeder, this latt still located just behind the bonnet grille and operated by the dashboard-piercing 'umbrella' gearchange lever, whi (among other things) allowed 'B-Eurocrats' to legislate this unforgettable classic out of production in the 1990s. At ov 8 million examples (including over 2 million vans), it was France's most prolific model ever.

enault Superfive TSE, 1985. Having sold millions of Fives, Renault followed that act with the Superfive, a same-but-
fferent car. It retained the cheeky chic of the Five, but it was updated comprehensively, with a transverse engine and
ve-speed gearbox (except on base models), better seats, dashboard and ergonomics. It looked sleeker and ran more
iietly and generally it remained supermini, as only the diesel, GTX and Monaco exceeded 1.5-litres. Enter yet another
enault million-plus best-seller, continuing into the 1990s, because in 'Campus' guise, like the Dauphine and the 4CV,
e Clio could not immediately replace the Superfive.

enault 25 V6 Turbo, 1985. Renault replaced their flagship 20/30 range with the aerodynamic (0.30 Cx) 25, which
ted for eight years. This was Renault's 'Turbo Period' and, while lesser models made do with the 20 TX's 2.2-litre,
gle ohc, four-cylinder engine, the top model boasted a turbocharged Douvrin PRV 2.5-litre, all-alloy, single ohc, V6
werplant, giving slingshot performance, coupled with sumptuous comfort. Heuliez custom-made a slightly stretched
ousine in two versions, of which fewer than 1,000 were sold, only 1 per cent of which were sold into the UK market.

Renault Espace, 1985. When Peugeot said 'non' to Matra's MPV prototype idea, it was rejigged using Renault parts a[nd] then presented to Renault, who promptly appreciated its true potential. In retrospect, the shape seems slightly angul[ar] but it was the unrivalled flexibility of the internal seating and space permutations which caught buyers' imaginations. A[dd] to that a galvanized steel separate chassis and coachwork skeleton to which composite panels were fixed, a sturd[y] 2.2-litre, single ohc, four-cylinder engine and gearbox lifted from the Renault 20 TX, Renault 25 GTX alloy road whee[ls] and *voilà*! Another Renault winner in a widely to be copied niche.

Renault Fuego Turbo, 1985. By the time Renault came to rejuvenate its Fuego coupé with a turbocharger, the barr[el] sided bodywork looked past its youthful best. The Phase Two Renault 18 bonnet modifications, cross-spoked, alloy ro[ad] wheels and an improved interior were allied to the higher performance engine, available for the contemporary, upgrade[d] turbocharged saloon, thus prolonging its marketability. As on the earlier model, the doors on this Fuego were opened [by] a little lever on the trailing edge, which the fingers accessed via a scalloped indentation in the bodywork, a somew[hat] controversial feature.

enault Alpine GTA V6 Turbo 'Europa Cup' Racer, 1986. To enhance its image as a high-tech company in the Formula One circus and to build a higher profile for its latest Alpine sports car, Renault negotiated for all Grands Prix of this year o be preceded by regulation-restricted versions of this vehicle. The racing, which superseded a similar Renault 5 Turbo eries, saw close and exciting battles between these sponsor-bespangled, plastic supercars from all over Europe, running n special wheels, giving tenacious roadholding, slingshot acceleration, an unforgettable whistling acceleration rumble d flame-spouting exhausts on the overrun.

enault 11 Turbo, 1987. Mark 2 11s (and 9s) sported a smooth front (flush light clusters, smaller air intakes and wind-eating plastic front bumper-cum-spoiler incorporating yellow foglamps), smooth plastic bodywork side skirts, vamped rear light layout with aerodynamic plastic bumper-cum-spoiler again and specific-to-model alloy road wheels. nis particular car illustrates Renault's experiments with four-wheel-steering, much in vogue at the time, but which was t pursued commercially. Note the number plate: 4 *Roues* (wheels) *Directrices* (steering) and regional code. Perhaps the imber-plate game is not a peculiarly British preserve?

Renault Medallion, 1987. In order to widen its range in the USA, Renault-AMC developed an Americanized Renault 21 named Medallion, which in saloon, hatchback and station-wagon forms were to be imported from 1987 and eventually to be assembled in America. An alternative was to manufacture in the joint Renault-Peugeot factory in Canada. The federalized revisions to the front necessitated a completely new front end – bumpers, grille, lights, wings and bonnet – with the concomitant underpinning modification and the rear, especially the bumpers, was beefed up, while the engines were 'de-smogged'. The centre section remained resolutely European. Renault's disposal of AMC to Chrysler foreshortened the range's sales life.

Renault 21 Monaco, 1987. With the exception of the 21 Turbo, this range, good though it was, never stood out from the crowd, so the Monaco treatment which was also applied to the Superfive and the 25 was a well-kept secret. Available only in metallic chocolate brown with discreet gold badging, the tan leather interior, complete with sunroof, made this a desirable machine for the sybarite. The wheel trims were specific to model, too.

Renault 21 4 x 4 Nevada, 1988. Only in the UK was the very popular estate version of Renault's 21 known as 'Savanna' and for some European countries with snowier climes, such as Switzerland, Austria and France, a 4 x 4 model (perfected by SINPAR, by then a subsidiary of SAVIEM, Renault's commercial arm at that time) was launched in three versions: TX (1995cc petrol, with or without catalytic converter) and GTD (2068cc diesel). A three-way, dashboard-mounted switch controlled the pneumatic engagement of the dog clutch to activate the rear wheels' propeller shaft, whose presence necessitated a small central floor tunnel.

Renault Mégane Concept Car, 1988. Wishing to consolidate their high-tech company image, Renault's dramatic V6-powered Paris Salon star bristled with innovative ideas. The doors slid apart towards their respective wheels and the front seats swivelled towards their respective doorways to ease accessibility; there were no exterior mirrors, rearward facing cameras relaying their views to interior TV screens; the rear seats were more like reclining armchairs and there was remote control central locking. The rear light panel presaged the Safrane's and the slippery shape, maximized by aerodynamic front and rear bumpers, gave a drag factor of 0.21.

Renault Espace, 1988. This brilliant concept of Matra had been successfully marketed and built by Renault and deman-
always exceeded production because the galvanized chassis and composite bodywork was not production-friendly
Towards the end of the decade, the sharpness of the original silhouette needed updating, so a softer front with bette
integrated auxiliary lights in the lip spoiler and colour coding all round, specific-to-model alloy road wheels and a
updated interior trim helped to freshen this masterly MPV. This is the top model, but a diesel version was still lacking o
the UK market.

Renault (Alpine) GTA 'Le Mans', 1989. The first of the special versions of Renault's prestige sports car was the 'L
Mans', which was being finalized in 1989, although it was not officially launched until the 1990 Geneva Show. It w;
based on the German 'Fleischmann' kit with bulging wheel arches, side valences and special colour-coded front and rea
bumpers (the front ones with integral fog lamps) and a modified front (transfer of wraparound flashers into the bumper
The engine was a catalysed version of the turbocharged V6 and the interior was leather (cloth for UK, where only thirt
five were sold). All had special wide, cross-spoke, specific-to-model, alloy road wheels.

CHAPTER TEN

THE INNOVATIVE NINETIES

Renault Scénic concept car, 1991. This concept car clearly illustrates Renault's pragmatism, coupled with forward thinking and innovation. It is another Patrick Le Quément star, featuring a sandwich floor construction and rain-repellent windscreen and yet it did not resemble a van. Five years later, in a less stylized form, the Mégane Scénic, slotting between the Twingo and the Espace, widened Renault's common-platform strategy and started the medium-sized MAC (multi-activity car) revolution, which other vehicle manufacturers fell over each other to emulate.

INTRODUCTION

By 1990, rationalization had made Renault slimmer and more competitive and it transmuted into a state-owned limited liability company. The Four and the Superfive were near the end of their commercial lives, a replacement for the Nineteen was in view and the need – already foreseen by Dreyfus in the 1950s – of international co-operation was ever-pressing.

With the liberalization of trade with the former Eastern Bloc, Renault/Volvo offered to buy Czechoslovakia's Skoda, but were refused, in favour of Volkswagen. Undeterred, Renault established 200 sales points in the former East Germany. Volvo and Renault were moving ever closer – a logical step, for the French company had already supplied more than 1 million engines to the Scandinavians' Dutch plant and Volvo had been distributing Renault vehicles throughout Scandinavia via their network for a long time. Despite considerable cross-shareholdings, Volvo became unable to complete the planned integration in September 1993 owing to the opposition of a group of Volvo shareholders and so another co-operative dream came to nothing.

The European Commission ruled that the French government's financial loan to Renault in 1988 to help the company out of difficulties was preferential and it required a major part of the amount to be promptly repaid, which was honoured. This financial burden coincided with the 1990 launch of Renault's next blockbuster, the Renault Clio range, the 1991 COTY winner. The following year, Renault launched its last Alpine, the A-610 Turbo and the second generation of the unchallenged Espace. With the fast-selling Nineteen and Clio, Renault became the best-selling imported marque in Germany.

In 1992 the company's emblem was updated, becoming a smoother *losange*. The company also introduced two new vehicles, the upmarket Safrane, replacing the Twenty-Five, and the cheeky, economical, monobox Twingo, which confirmed the company's pre-eminence for innovation. The year also saw Louis Schweitzer take over from Raymond Lévy at the helm of Renault and the company became the majority shareholder in Turkey's Oyak-Renault, while manufacture ceased in Louis' beloved Billancourt.

Renault finally bade farewell to the inimitable Four and claimed the world champion constructors' title (with Williams-Renault) and the world champion driver's title (with Nigel Mansell) during the same year, both these championships being annexed in the following year, thanks to Alain Prost.

Patrick Le Quément's design department at Renault continued to win the admiration of the car industry and the public alike with project/concept cars foreshadowing aspects of production cars – Laguna, Scénic, Racoon, the Ludo and Modus city cars, Initiale, Argos, Pangea and Zo.

In 1994, the Laguna superseded the Twenty-One and later became British Touring Car Championship saloon car winner. With the eventual fading of the Superfive in 1995 and the Mégane family replacing the Nineteen in 1996, the last of the numbers disappeared from Renault's line-up and Renault offered one of the youngest passenger vehicle ranges. Models continued to pour forth: the Sport Spider, the Grand Espace, the Kangoo, Clio II and, especially, the clever Scénic (MAC) variant of the Mégane's platform, which joined the hatch, the Classic (saloon), the coupé and the convertible with an estate version in the wings. This successful common-base technology was the envy of other European manufacturers.

Fifty years after the French government had expropriated Louis' company from the private sector into public ownership, it oversaw a successful partial reprivatization of this profitable state organization; the wheel had turned almost full circle. The year's end saw the passing of Pierre Dreyfus, la Régie's retired, successful captain for twenty years, and Renault finally erased the totality of its financial debts.

In this decade, apart from Formula One, in which Renault-engined cars won more Grands Prix than any other manufacturer's, the company continued its active support of grass-roots competition (small saloons such as Clio), of high profile championships (such as 'tintop' racing with Laguna), rallying (with Maxi Clios and Maxi Méganes) and single-seater divisions (Formula Renault). To capitalize on this technological commitment, Renault offered class-leading models, including the Superfive GT Turbo 'Raider', the Clio 16V, the (three special editions of the) Clio Williams, the Sport Spider and the Safrane Biturbo (not available in the UK).

The company continued practical experimentation with alternative fuels, notably electric power which was used to power a fleet of special 'plug-in' Clios in the full-scale commuter transport 'Praxitèle' project in Quentin-en-Yvelines and some of their top production models were available with computerized, voice-synthesized, on-board, satellite-positioned, video navigation systems. Safety improvements were offered continuously on their cars (air bags, programmed safety restraints, anti-lock brakes, etc.) and direct-injection diesel engines, which significantly improved existing, proven, oil-burning power units' frugality while lowering their pollutants, were series-introduced in 1998.

Despite the increasingly worldwide governmental restrictions on vehicle requirements, Renault continued on a positive path, with engine/transmission unit supply to an Indian partner, with increasing van manufacture in China and similar joint production with GM in Europe (where GM's Arena-badged Trafic replaced the Midi). They arranged diesel engine supply to South Korean manufacturers and made plans to revive parts of the ailing Russian vehicle-manufacturing industry through joint ventures, besides reinforcing their already significant presence throughout the South American market (Mercosur), particularly in Colombia and Argentina (with large 'exports' to Brazil), which they deemed to be more important and less financially demanding than the long-term investment necessary in the financially unstable Far Eastern markets, a particularly perspicacious decision.

The company's participation as the most successful engine supplier in Formula One for nearly a decade gained it enormous publicity in terms of being widely perceived as a forward-looking, high-tech organization. But to be an undisputed champion indefinitely offers diminishing returns and, thus, Renault withdraw from the highest ranks of motor racing, having been world champion six times (1992–7 inclusive), to conquer new fields, such as aeronautics, where they introduced a completely new family of lightweight aero engines.

Approaching its centennial birthday, the Renault organization remains in the top flight of world manufacturers – of engines, of robotic industrial tools and of cars, commercial vehicles and railroad equipment – and with a reputation of which Louis Renault himself would have been very proud.

Renault 21 Turbo, 1990. Late in the Renault 21's life cycle there came a real flyer, complete with all the comforts and gadgets expected of a Ford Cosworth challenger, including a 'Quadra' four-wheel-drive version. Available only as a four-door saloon, its longitudinally located 2-litre turbocharged engine was quiet and efficient and the alloy road wheels, boot spoiler and colour-coded bumpers were specific to model. But – as for its performance peers – high insurance premiums posed problems, even if the considerable price tag was no deterrent, so it did not sell in significant numbers, in spite of its attractive specification.

Renault Laguna Concept Car, 1990. This was a Patrick Le Quément project which foreshadowed a number of features later to appear on the Renault Sport Spider, such as the transverse mid-mounted engine, although, in this case, it came from the 2-litre 21 Turbo and there was a wind-deflector rather than a windscreen, while the front and back ends had a great similarity. First shown in October 1990, the striking lines, metallic blue paintwork, imaginative interior and unusual wheel stylers made this a regular centre of attraction at motor shows.

Renault 19 16-Valve, 1991. Renault's 120mph plus version of the 19 had sixteen valves, being available as a saloon, a hatchback and, later, as a four-seater convertible. It boasted a macho NACA duct on its bonnet, deep, specific-to-model, aerodynamic, front bumper-cum-spoiler with a flexible lower lip, wind-cheating body side-skirts, lowered suspension, unusual alloy road wheels with low profile tyres and a tail spoiler. Internally, there were bolstered bucket front seats (black leather optional), leather-rimmed steering wheel and gearknob and electric tinted windows. The hatchback was a three-door and the saloon a four-door version.

Renault Clio 1.4 RT, 1991. Renault's Clio was their competitive riposte to Peugeot's 205 and the transverse engine placement, highly effective noise suppression and top quality interior fittings helped the car to become Car of the Year for 1991. With a choice of three or five doors, three petrol engines and a diesel, with three trim levels, Clio — aided by 'Nicole' and 'Papa' in the UK — sent Renault's British sales rocketing. A rigid bodyshell, supple ride, eager handling and better rust protection won many admirers, who overlooked the less than perfect seating position. But those top-model, alloy road wheels were real finger wreckers!

Renault Clio 16V, 1992. As the Renault Superfive aged, so the Clio became Renault UK's most popular range, powerfully promoted on TV by 'Nicole'. The purposeful sixteen-valve attracted drivers – often those upgrading from the Superfive GT Turbo pocket rocket – through the smoothness of the new engine, suave interior, comprehensive instrumentation and specific-to-model, alloy road wheels, shrouded by muscular-looking, deformable composite front wings, which all added up to a class-leading, very price-competitive yet insurance-affordable package. Later versions adopted the five-spoke alloy road wheels of the Renault 19 16V.

Renault Twingo, 1993. To supplement the *monocorps* (single box) Espace, Renault launched on an unsuspecting public Patrick Le Quément's 1.2-litre, five-speed, single-trim-level Twingo. This cheeky newcomer was eagerly accepted and it was never out of the top-five best-sellers because it offered economy of purchase, maintenance and operation, combined with comfort, astonishing space and seating versatility, not to mention its *art nouveau* interior and digital instruments. To Brits' chagrin, this pert *gamine* (youngster) was not available in a right-hand-drive version, although many still crossed the Channel permanently.

Renault 19, 1993. The saloon version in Renault's 19 range was initially named 'Chamade', but another manufacturer's complaint of a similarity of name caused its withdrawal. The 'Chamade' appellation was affixed to the rear boot lid, opposite Renault 19, so its absence on the vehicle illustrated (combined with the lights cluster across the lower lip) identifies this as a top-specification, Phase Two version, which offered alloy road wheels, electric tinted windows, glass sunroof and, internally, velour trim with headrests all round. By some months, the saloon was outlived on the British market by its hatchback counterpart.

Renault Clio Williams, 1993. Although it was entirely a French confection, Renault played on their Formula One Grand Prix success with Frank Williams through this 2-litre, limited edition hatchback. It was a class ultimate, with a 150bhp transverse engine, exclusive blue finish (inside and out), series number plaque (on the dashboard) for the first series, gold 'Speedline' alloy road wheels and special coachwork graphics. It went like greased lightning with incredible ease, eclipsing even its class-leading sixteen-valve sister. All three versions were instant classics, with virtually nil depreciation, and it remains today an icon of the 1990s.

Renault Safrane, 1994. This smooth, executive-market hatchback appeared more like its 'nostrilled' sister, Laguna, than its preceding 25, but it inherited much of that range's power plant and running gear, although the powerful Biturbo version was never offered in the UK. The Safrane continued the 25's considerable sales success in continental Europe (an achievement sadly not mirrored on the British market), remaining continually near the top of its class. There was a revamp for the 1997 model year, which included new front and rear bodywork, and the top version used a five-cylinder engine, also found in contemporary Volvos.

Renault 19 16V Cabriolet, 1994. Draconian American automobile regulations had threatened to legislate open-topped cars into extinction, but this did not happen and roadsters and cabriolets made a comeback in the late 1980s and '90s. The 19 Mark 2 ('nostrilled' grille with new bonnet, modified front spoiler-cum-bumper, suaver alloy road wheels, neater aerodynamic body side mouldings and revised rear end), seen here, was a felicitous offering, taking particularly kindly to Karmann's 'chop top' treatment and the unusual double-bump rear head fairings, which helped to disguise successfully the heavy duty folded soft top. It gave way to its Mégane sibling, with which there was a noticeable family likeness.

Renault Ludo, 1994. This was the company's concept of a four-seater city saloon, using a catalyst-equipped, LPG-powered engine, with an automatic clutch, energy efficient tyres on alloy wheels and 'Carminat' traffic navigation system. On the vehicle's right, the doors slid open from the middle (no centre pillar) and there was a single trailing-hinged driver's door; it had four-position seats and many interior touches derived from the Twingo. The double curvature rear screen reappeared on Renault's Clio II and doubtless other cues will be incorporated in future Renaults.

Renault Argos Concept Car, 1994. If Ludo expounded Renault's ideas on the future of city vehicles, then Argos, l'esprit nouveau (new spirit), illustrated Patrick Le Quément's thoughts on a sports car, which rejected the 'bio design' which aerodynamic efficiency was stamping on cars' shapes. It was based on an extended Twingo floorpan, together with its simple, transverse, ohv, catalysed engine and five-speed gearbox, which was controlled by a dashboard-mounted, electronically actuated gear shift, and the unusual, three-seater layout was staggered. The shape was meant to be simple yet memorable, with deliberately exposed bolt heads but, to many, it was just rather quirky.

Renault Initiale, 1995. Another stunning Patrick Le Quément show car, the Initiale gave styling cues to Renault's forthcoming super luxury cars. This four-seater featured a Formula One 3500cc V10 engine detuned to 392bhp, an automatic clutch for the six-speed, sequentially controlled gearbox, giving four-wheel-drive. The tinted glazing encompassed windscreen, roof and a complex-opening rear V-hatch, enclosing Louis Vuitton designer luggage. It had an intelligent electronic speed regulator which reacted to traffic flow to minimize accidents, and the Scottish leather-finished interior was fitted with the latest IT gizmos, novel instrumentation and on-board laser-disc film entertainment.

Renault Sport Spider, 1996. When Renault first proposed this radical two-seater, it had a minimalist, but stylish, interior, an extruded aluminium chassis and composite panels, the whole being powered by a transverse, mid-located, ex-Clio Williams, 150bhp, sixteen-valve engine. The first version, which raced all over Europe in a one-make championship, had a curious but efficient air deflector, which was supplemented in 1996 with the windscreen and small front wind deflectors seen here. Manufactured at the Alpine works in Dieppe, it was later developed for publicity purposes to run on LPG, ex rally ace Jean Ragnotti at the wheel.

Renault Light Aircraft Engine, 1997. Having conquered Formula One with their engines, Renault looked around for new fields to develop. Expertise in extracting maximum efficiency from a given power unit led the company naturally back into the aero-engine field, in which Renault had been pre-eminent almost throughout Louis' reign. Instead of avgas, the generally utilized and noticeably polluting aviation fuel, the Renault engines ran on more environmentally friendly paraffin, thus improving reliability, reducing noise and stretching service intervals by up to 50 per cent. The engines ranged from 180 to 300bhp and had an excellent power/altitude ratio of performance.

Renault Mégane Range, 1997. With the launch of the Mégane hatchback in 1996, Renault began to replace the Renault 19 range at a rate which confounded competitors. In quick succession, there appeared a coupé, a saloon (the Classic), a soft-top convertible and a ground-breaking multi-activity car (the Scénic), all based on a common floorpan and a variety of engines. In 1998, the Society of Motor Manufacturers & Traders confirmed the astonishing fact that the Mégane range had outsold every other model on the UK market during April, the first time ever that a foreign car had bested Ford, Vauxhall or Rover.

Renault Clio II RXE, 1998. The original highly successful Clio had undergone three updatings before it was superseded by a slightly larger and sharper-looking range, in which the various models included virtually all the extras which the market demanded at a price lower than that of the outgoing equivalents. This resulted in an excellent initial sales take-up, similar to the record-breaking sales which the Mégane had achieved. The cars had an unmistakable double curvature rear screen, composite front wings, an aluminium bonnet and plastic-lensed front lights and were quickly offered with the new, very economical, direct-injection diesel engines which Renault had introduced recently on the Mégane range.

Renault Zo Concept Car, 1998. Under Patrick Le Quément's influence, Renault had become famous for concept cars – Mégane, Laguna, Scénic, Zoom, Racoon, Argos, Initiale and others. At the 1998 Geneva Salon, Renault presented a centennial offering, Zo, a three-seater all-terrain leisure vehicle using the Sport Spider's modular aluminium chassis and powered by Europe's first direct-injection petrol engine coupled to an automatic transmission. The driver sat in the middle, protected by an air deflector, and the interior was minimalist. It was a confirmation of Renault's inventive approach to motoring for the new millennium.

THE ALPINE CONNECTION

Alpine A-106 Cabriolet, 1957. To widen the Alpine range away from the competition-oriented Coupé 'Mille Miles', Jean Rédélé had Michelotti produce a very smart soft-top vehicle with a handsome front and a back which was the forerunner of that found later on Renault's Ghia-designed Floride. The 4CV ancestry is plain to see and only two were built, one a standard 4CV with three-speed gearbox and the other a tuned one, for Jean Galtier. When productionized the following year with a plastic body from Chappe Frères, there were a number of visible frontal differences and plate wheels were standard.

INTRODUCTION

Born in 1922 in Dieppe, Jean was the eldest son of Emil Rédélé, erstwhile Billancourt competitions mechanic, who had set up a taxi and bus servicing business between the two world wars before taking on the Renault agency; it was in these workshops that young Jean had spent much of his youth. By 1947, having gained his HEC diploma (*Hautes Etudes Commerciales* – Advanced Business Studies), he took charge of the war-damaged enterprise, becoming the youngest French Renault concessionaire. To re-establish the business in a vehicle-starved era, he started dealing in second-hand cars and refurbishing ex-American army lorries which were then sold throughout France and overseas. Jean drove all over the country locating and bringing home spare parts, travelling which stood him in good stead later when he rallied a 4CV all over the country. While he successfully drove an R-1062 and then an R-1063 in all sorts of events, such as Le Mans, the Mille Miglia, the Monte Carlo Rally, the Liège–Rome–Liège, as well as running the Grands Garages Normands, he dreamed of building his own Renault-based sports car.

His first Michelotti-designed, Allemano-built 'Renault Spéciale', a two-seater sports coupé, won the 1953 Dieppe Rally outright on its maiden appearance. At the time, with his co-pilot Louis Pons, he bought the rights to manufacture the Georges Claude five-speed gearbox, based on the 4CV's three-speed casing. Renault had previously declined this project, but was nevertheless Rédélé's first customer for use in their 'hot' 4CV, the R-1063!

The second sports car, the first 'Rédélé Spéciale' was completed in Italy and collected by Jean during his honeymoon in December 1952, but it needed much fettling. Therefore a third sports car was manufactured, the 'Marquis' car, later shown at the New York Motor Show, for which a manufacturing licence was sold to an American industrialist, Zark Reed, although the whole enterprise turned out badly.

Next, Rédélé persuaded the Chappe brothers, coachbuilders of St-Maur, to manufacture in metal a different sports coupé to another Michelotti design. When this was completed it was used as a buck, from which a series of moulds were taken, allowing the production of a number of glassfibre-reinforced, polyester resin bodies. These were ferried to Alpine's Paris location (Charles Escoffier, Paris Renault agent in rue Forest, was Jean's father-in-law) to be mounted on a strengthened 4CV chassis, thus becoming the first production Alpine, the A-106 coupé, alongside which a graceful Michelotti-inspired convertible was added in 1958.

The A-108 range (coupé, convertible and fixed head) was based on a strengthened Dauphine chassis with a Dauphine-Gordini engine and appeared next in parallel to the A-106 models, but it later had a tubular chassis for the coachwork to clothe and, in 1960, the first of the so-called 'Berlinette' bodies appeared together with a gawky 2 + 2 coupé.

A bewildering combination of models were sold over the following decade, including the four-seater GT4, but it is probably the A-110/1300G and 1600S which are the best known through their many competition exploits. Manufacturing licences were successfully sold to Willys do Brasil (Interlagos), Dina in Mexico (Dinalpine), FASA in Spain (Alpine) and Bulgarenault in Bulgaria (Bulgaralpine) and hundreds were sold worldwide during the 1960s.

The astute Rédélé saw the advantages of moving upmarket and, in 1971, at the Geneva Show, he launched the A-310, using the four-cylinder Renault Sixteen TX 1605cc engine, enclosed in a completely new Belligond-designed luxury 2 + 2 (plastic) body. The co-incidence of warranty claims (electrics) and the fuel crisis caused financial problems at Alpine and, in 1973, Renault took a major share in the company. They eventually took over total control in 1977 when the trusty all-alloy engine was replaced by the Douvrin PRV6 to make the car a refined GT sports car, and assembly of the Five Alpine (Gordini) was undertaken by the specialized workforce at Dieppe. Lotus used five A-310/V6s as mules to carry out component testing for De Lorean's forthcoming DMC3 coupé.

In 1979, the ex-Renault Thirty five-speed gearbox became standard on the A-310/V6, which, two years later, was revised body-wise to accommodate the Renault Five Turbo suspension and wheels. The mid-engined Monte Carlo Rally winning Renault Five Turbo was built in the same workshops throughout its life (including the Turbo Two and Maxi Turbo versions), as were the Five Alpine (Gordini) Turbo and 'Coupe' versions of the Superfive GT Turbo Marks 1 and 2, not to mention the innovative Matra-designed Espace.

At the 1985 Geneva Show, Renault replaced the A-310/V6 with the Alpine V6 GT and V6 Turbo (called Renault GTA in the UK). The previous model, following A-110 practice, had used a large diameter, single tube backbone chassis to which was affixed the strong coachwork carcase with strengthened stress points. The new cars, however, were based on a fabricated steel spine to which all the plastic panels were glued with adhesives having the same modulus of elasticity as the panels themselves, thus ensuring that, after heat curing, the whole had virtually the same torsional strength as a true monocoque (single structure).

The 'Americanization' modifications, which Dieppe made to the V6 Turbo prior to Renault selling AMC to Chrysler and aborting the whole project, were incorporated in the succeeding Alpine/Renault A-610 Turbo, notably the 'pop up' headlights. This mature, rapid and comparatively inexpensive GT car could not be saved by replacing the Renault diamond on its nose by an Alpine roundel. It disappeared in 1994, the last of the Alpine marque – at least for the twentieth century – and the Espace filled the production void. Later, Renault's Sport Spider would be assembled here.

Alpine was world rally champion in 1973 and also produced successful Formula Two, Formula Three, Formula Renault and Formula France single-seaters and the A500, the laboratory forerunner of Renault's own Formula One car. At Le Mans, Alpine won both Class and Index honours and was very much involved with the 1978 outright winner.

Alpine's wealth of competition experience and enthusiasm smoothed Renault's passage to the forefront of motorsport and today has a loyal, worldwide following, especially in France, Germany and Japan.

Alpine A-106 'Mille Miles' Coupé, 1955. Pierre Dreyfus, then head of the RNUR, is introduced to the first series-produced cars by the marque's founder, Jean Rédélé, who is just visible in the driver's seat. This is the red one of the deliberately *tricouleur* trio (the white and blue ones are reflected in the polished coachwork), which had been drawn up in a row for evaluation by Renault's directors in the factory's famous cobbled square, surrounding the garden in which Louis Renault's original shed at Billancourt stands to this very day. On cost grounds, the Frégate rear screen forms the windscreen and the vehicle is based on the 4CV's punt chassis, engine and transmission.

Alpine Allemano Prototype, 1959. It was thought that this Dauphine-based, steel-bodied, fixed-head coupé might succeed the Alpine A-106. It retained the earlier 'star fixing' road wheels, but had a smooth front with frenched-in headlamps and sidelights below, and hip-located air scoops; the rear deck, which hid a 998cc 'Ventoux'-based engine and four-speed gearbox, was hinged at the rear screen base and a raised moulding ran down the centre with 'ALPINE' across the trailing edge as it sloped away between small rear fins to a Kamm-type rear grille with inset Floride rear lights. This little-known and misnamed 'A-107' remained unique.

Alpine A-108 Sports Coupé, 1960. This year's production was the first to incorporate a backbone chassis to which the bodywork was bonded, the coupé being a cabriolet with an integrally built hard-top. The water and fuel filler caps were on the rear decking behind the rear screen and the Dauphine-Gordini engine with four-speed gearbox remained the most popular version of this model. Introduced at the 1959 Paris Salon, this Michelotti-penned model, with classical nose, gave way to the 'shark nose' Berlinette front at the following Salon, although the tail always remained unchanged, until this model disappeared in 1964.

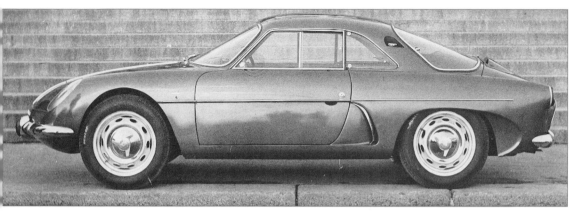

Alpine A-108 Berlinette 'Tour de France', 1960. Presented at the 1960 Paris Salon, this is recognizably the forerunner of Alpine's most famous car. But it still had the 'Ventoux' engine at the back, which required air scoops in front of the back wheels for cooling and a filler (one for fuel, one for water) on each rear quarter at head level. The bonnet scoops are plain to see and the rear grille was as on the earlier cabriolet. Engine sizes were 845cc, 904cc, or 998cc, with four- or five-speed gearboxes to choose from, all mounted on a single tubular backbone chassis and clothed with glass-fibre reinforced plastic coachwork.

Alpine A-110L GT4, 1966. As the old A-108 2 + 2 began to look *passé*, Alpine's bodymakers, Chappe Frères, combined the front of the previous model with a new, less angular four-seater body. The GT4 was hardly elegant, but it was exclusive and allowed fanatical Alpine families to drive their favourite marque. This model was always built with the 'Sierra' five-main-bearing engine and four-speed gearbox, and L signified 'long' (chassis), which was 10cm longer than the older A-108 2 + 2 (already 7 cm longer than the Berlinette). More than 110 were built between 1964 and 1969.

Alpine Experimental Sportster, 1968. Jean Rédélé was ever an imaginative thinker and, through Alpine Engineering, OSI of Turin, built a prototype using a Cycolac CRV body shell, similar to that clothing a Chevrolet Corvair prototype. A reinforced polyester chassis used a 60bhp Renault 'Sierra' engine and Renault Eight gearbox, suspension and wheels, the clamshell bottom and top (note the joining strip running round) enclosing the whole, while the interior was all washable plastic. The hump on the tail allowed engine clearance and the front panel hinges are 4CV ones. The chassis/body ensemble weighed only 200 kg and this leisure vehicle remains unique.

Alpine A-110/1600 S Berlinette, 1968. This is the ill-fated car of Gérard Larrousse and Marcel Callewaert in the snowy mountains while competing in the 1968 Monte Carlo Rally, before tragedy struck. While leading the event, Larrousse, in the Col de Turini, approached a bend, absolutely flat out. The road surface was meant to be dry, but some idiots had thrown snow all over the dangerous bends 'to liven things up a bit'. The racing tyres lost their grip, the car went out of control and was smashed beyond repair and so months of preparation and a likely win were pointlessly thrown away.

Alpine-Renault A-310/4, 1971. The success of the A-110 Berlinette did not blind Jean Rédélé to his marque's future. From one of his sketches, Marcel Belligond of Renault's Styling Centre realized this prototype car, which, for homologation purposes, suppressed the just visible slotted rear screen mask and changed the body-integrated rear light clusters above the rear rubbing strip for Renault 17 parts below. Otherwise unchanged, it was introduced at the 1972 Geneva Salon with six headlights behind plexiglass and a 1605cc 140bhp engine, using the same production techniques as its smaller predecessor.

Alpine A-210 (M66), 1966. Renault's climb to Le Mans supremacy in 1978 was launched by Jean Rédélé's indomitable determination to conquer *le circuit sarthois* with his Len Terry-designed M63. Three years later, 1300cc A-210s took the first three places in the Index of Thermal Efficiency; the winner is seen here being driven by Jacques Cheinisse and Roger de Langeneste. The Gordini-designed engines had twin-cam, crossflow, aluminium cylinder heads, fed by twin Weber 45 DCOE carburettors and transistorized ignition. A Porsche gearbox replaced the previously fragile Hewland unit and the significantly modified long-travel suspension allowed an underbody fairing.

Alpine A-364 Formula Three Racer, 1972. When automobile industry newcomers Matra 'won' the loan that the French government offered to enable a French firm to build a world-beating Formula One car, despite Alpine's Renault-based proven competition history, Jean Rédélé vowed to oppose them in all forms of motorsport and to win. The car seen here is but one of his successful *monoplace* (single-seater) confections, nicknamed 'Dinosaur', because of its aerodynamically efficient, slotted engine cover. Dudot (left) was the engine wizard (he was later Renault's Formula One top engine man), de Cortanze (centre) was the chassis man and Hubert was the aerodynamics boss.

CHAPTER TWELVE

THE OTHER RENAULTS

Autobleu Coupé, 1957. Autobleu was Renault's major tuning equipment supplier for over twenty years. In 1952, MM. Mestivier and Lepeytre, the proprietors, commissioned from Luigi Segre of Ghia a coupé body on a 4CV chassis, which they exhibited to la Régie, which is how those two parties were introduced. The engine with 'pipe Autobleu' and standard running gear was exclusive but expensive, and it was slow getting into production (the first one was delivered in November 1955), initially with Ghia then with Figioni and finally with Henri Chapron, who also offered a cabriolet version (only two produced). Approximately eighty were manufactured up to early 1957.

INTRODUCTION

In the same way that vehicle makers have always utilized components manufactured by other companies, such as tyres, electrical equipment, etc., so other car makers, amateurs and coachbuilders have used Renault components to create different vehicles. In Louis' time, the only significant example was SAPRAR (Société Anonyme de Pièces de Rechange d'Automobiles Renault), a Renault subsidiary, who, at the end of the 1930s, offered a very small number of SAPRAR Sports, clothed as a Darl'Mat-type, Partout-manufactured, two-seater convertible.

The destruction wrought by the Second World War was more widespread than that of the First World War and included damage to many requisitioned civilian vehicles. The scarcity of new cars, coupled with the mechanical 'handiness' of more people, led to an industry reassembling different components into 'specials', perhaps best illustrated by the Austin Seven and Ford Ten specials in the UK. In France, although Panhard and Citroën parts were used, Renault components were most widely utilized. Space does not permit an in-depth history of all of these, but an allusion is made to most.

The most famous Renault-based marque was Alpine, whose history has already been detailed. Of the high profile marques, the abortive USA-inspired, Belfast-built De Lorean DMC sports car, using the Douvrin-built PRV six-cylinder engine and gearbox 'bloc' was the most notorious. Colin Chapman's Lotus Europa utilized the four-cylinder unit from the Renault Sixteen together with its gearbox.

Atla was an early 4CV-based fibre glass, two-seat, gullwing coupé using a tubular space frame and made in very small numbers in a Parisian suburb. Fewer than twelve units are believed to have been manufactured.

Brissonneau et Lotz of Montataire productionized a 'civilized', fibre glass-reinforced, plastic-bodied version of Louis Rosier's Le Mans *barquette*. A pretty vehicle based on the 4CV, it metamorphosed through two versions, until its final year, when a cutaway-door version was also offered. The company abandoned the project after some 200 examples, when it won the contract to produce the Floride's body for Renault. A licence to produce a plastic, door-less version as 'the Rogue' was also granted to Plasticar of Doylestown, Pa., but series-manufacture never materialized.

Henri Chapron was one of the leading French coachbuilders. The company took over the production of the Autobleu coupé from Figioni (see p. 151), and offered coupé and cabriolet versions of the 4CV-based 'Mouette' and 'Racing', sold in small numbers. Chapron also produced seven Frégate cabriolets and, by cutting out part of the roof, fitted a small number of Dauphines with a complete roll-back top like Renault's own 4CV *décapotable*.

The BSH (François Benais and Max Saint-Hilaire), a Kamm-tailed fibre glass coupé built by Marland, utilized either Eight Gordini, Twelve or Sixteen components and ran up a production total of about 200, before closing in 1973.

Mario Marsonetto, a Lyonnais *garagiste* (garage owner), first built a handful of 4CV-based 'Luciole' specials between 1957 and 1959. In 1965 he returned with an Eight-based, fibre glass, front-wheel-drive, four-seater coupé and, at the 1968 Paris Salon, followed this up with a Sixteen-based, 125mph version, modified at the back with a huge plexiglas hatch and five-speed gearbox, of which four were manufactured.

Jean-Emile Vernet and Jean Pairard inspired the Antem-clothed, mid-engined Renault R-1064 'Tank', which captured eight world records at Montlhéry in 1952. For the 1953 Le Mans 24 Hour Race, they entered a star-wheeled, high, fixed-head coupé derivative and, later that year, a 'civilized' version was commercialized in minute numbers as the VP Coupé.

The American-initiated, Volkswagen-based beach buggy craze spawned at least one Renault-based equivalent, the Buffalo, the fibre glass tub of which was bolted to a tubular chassis (not a Renault floor) and then the builder tacked on all the parts from any scrapped Dauphine or Eight. The kits came complete for self-assembly and, with a carefully chosen amalgam of parts, including a 1296cc Gordini engine, the company's boss, Roland Beilé, won the 1971 National Slalom finals in Strasbourg, beating seventy other keen competitors.

The Canadian-built Manic (from the indigenous Indian-named Manicaguan river) was the brainchild of Gérard About, who had been in charge of a project in the 1960s for Renault in Canada to evaluate the North American sales possibilities for Jean Rédélé's Renault-based Alpine A-110. Despite the corporation's rejection of his positive report, About was passionate that the project was viable so he resigned and eventually productionized his interpretation of the *berlinette*, based on a Renault Ten floor structure to which a Jidé-style plastic body (see p. 157) was attached. Performance was similar to the Alpine. Despite backing from the international Bombardier group, the project foundered after a production run of over one hundred units owing to insurmountable problems over Renault component supply. A collectable rarity, chassis rust has decimated survivors.

The Fournier-Marcardier bore the names of the founding Lyonnais enthusiasts of this Lotus-looking two-seater sports *barquette* utilizing Renault components. The vehicle was a *mid*-engined, artisanal, multi-tubular confection, for which a one-make championship ran for a couple of years in the late 1960s. It used Renault Eight running gear and suspension and was clothed in a plastic body. Production is unauthenticated but it is believed to have been about fifty, including the later Barzoï coupé.

GRAC, with whom About of Manic fame (see above) had some commercial links, was another artisanal marque, known also for its single-seater racing cars in Formula France. Often using Renault components, chiefly engines and gearboxes in tubular chassis, GRAC built some very attractive Chevron-esque coupés, but total production figures are difficult to validate owing to the diverse nature of the manufactures.

Briefly, Renault components contributed to all the following: Legros (coupé and *barquette*); Allemano (a Dauphine-based coupé); Graber (a 1958 modified Dauphine); Zagato (a 1957 coupé); Motto (maker of Louis Rosier's original GT coupé); GFH (another 4CV-based Motto coupé) as well as various vehicles by Mialle, Splendilux, La Chapelle, Chappe, JCB, Pichon-Parat, Labourdette, DB, Elina, Seaton, Scora, Poncin, Matra, Gruau, Colucci, Calmette, Llandeli, Heuliez, Boano, Duriez, Antem, Crespi, CAM, Polycarters, Bertin, Gamaches, Charbonneaux, Léotard, Chalmette and many others.

Rosier 4CV Barquette, 1953. Racing ace Louis Rosier was a Renault agent in Clermont-Ferrand and a keen 4CV driver. In 1952, he had Motto, the Turin coachbuilder, construct a svelte little two-seater aluminium coupé on a 4CV floorpan, which, unfortunately, proved too expensive to productionize. From that coupé, he produced this beautiful sports two-seater which ran at Le Mans in 1953, driven by his son, Jean-Louis, and Schollemann, finishing twenty-third overall. This car later formed the basis of the Brissonneau et Lotz sports car and Rosier also had a coupé built on a Frégate floorpan.

Ferry Renault Barquette, 1955. Pierre Ferry, a Renault 4CV engine tuning wizard, built for an enthusiastic fanatic, Blaché, this single-seater, which had two main chassis members, a highly tuned 904cc 'Ventoux' engine at the front, driving through an adapted 4CV gearbox to a special rear differential, turning the cast-alloy wheels via 4CV half axles. The aluminium coachwork was supported on lightweight tubes and the engine was fed by a twin-choke, downdraught Weber carburettor, producing 60bhp to give a top speed of over 110mph. This car has recently been discovered in, and rescued from, a Californian scrapyard!

René Bonnet Djet, 1963. When René Bonnet and Charles Deutsch, the partners in the DB concern, parted in 1962, the former started to base his cars on Renault instead of Panhard parts. For this vehicle, the world's first series-produced mid-engined coupé, Bonnet utilized a tuned 1108cc Renault 'Sierra' five-main-bearing engine driving the rear wheels through a four-speed Estafette gearbox. Production cars had a separate, single tube, backbone chassis with bolted-on fibre glass reinforced plastic coachwork; the 'bubble' rear screen opened backwards. Matra took over the ailing firm in 1964 and continued to manufacture updated versions (Djet V, Djet VS and Jet 6) up to 1968.

Ghia Renault R8 Coupé, 1964. Renault, originally through Luigi Segre, always had a special relationship with Ghia, illustrated through the batch of 4CV-based leisure vehicles (see p. 92), the 1957 Dauphine Sport and the Floride. At the Turin Show, this coachbuilder exhibited a remarkable metallic blue 'dragonfly window' sports car, based on a shortened and strengthened 8 chassis with the standard running gear, the Gordini mechanicals being offered as an option. The interior was completely coachbuilt with comprehensive instrumentation, grouped ahead of the driver, and a Nardi steering wheel. Note the flowing swage lines, the drilled (standard) hub caps and neat air extractor. This unique model is now owned by the original designer.

SOVAM Sports, 1968. This vehicle's manufacturer, from Parthenay, built strange-looking, airport servicing vehicles and mobile shops, which were sold Europe-wide. In 1965, the company brought out a front-wheel-drive, fibre-glass reinforced, plastic sports car, based on the Renault 4 floorpan, offering either a 45bhp 'Ventoux' engine or the Caravelle 1108cc 'Sierra' power plant. One example successfully completed a Paris–Calcutta–Paris journey in 1966, but two years later the starter model disappeared and the Eight Gordini-powered model was added. Its unusual appearance and an uncertain market persuaded the firm to return to its successful and profitable roots after making only a few hundred cars of which a handful survive.

Méan Sonora, 1969. Jacques d'Heur was the power behind this Belgian sports car from Havelange, the company producing an unusual polyester, two-seat, multi-part body, mounted on multi-tube spaceframe chassis, which was capable of accepting proprietary parts from many makes, notably Renault. The most popular configuration was a mid-mounted 'Sierra' engine with following gearbox and complete Renault 8 front suspension, but the Gordini 8 or 16 engine were alternatives and there was a targa top to fit between the windscreen rail and the rear roll-over bar-cum-backscreen. Roughly 200 kits were sold in this configuration. The Spa–Francorchamps circuit in Belgium is seen in the background.

Apal-Muschang-Renault, 1969. Léopold Muschang was a Renault concessionaire at Arlon in Belgium. He built a formidable twin-engined, four-wheel-drive, cross-country, competition vehicle based on a strengthened 4 chassis, with a fibre-glass open body; the front engine was a tuned 45bhp Renault 6 unit and the rear one was a tuned 75bhp Renault 8 S unit, each having its own gearbox. In conjunction with Apal, the well-known fibre-glass specialists, he commercialized a more sober, front-wheel-drive, plastic-bodied machine, here seen at the 1969 Brussels Motor Show, with seats, bumpers and lights from the 4.

Jidé, 1969. Jacques Durand was a specialist in fibre-glass-reinforced mouldings and was also an ardent sports car fanatic. He was one of the first and most successful small-scale manufacturers, using a simple multi-tubular chassis with Renault components such as 8 front cross-member and steering and engine/transmission ensemble and rear suspension. The body was not very elegant, but it was strong, could be bought as a kit, utilized a Floride windscreen and 8 Gordini mechanicals (later 12 and 16 units, mid-mounted in a special cradle). Production quantity is unknown, but kits were sold into the 1990s.

Suncar Arpège Roadster, 1982. The Département des Mines' regulations virtually killed off the 'specials' boom of the 1960s in France; in the 1980s this Annéçois firm offered a Renault 5 TS-based 'retro' convertible. Everything could be used from a donor car except the monocoque body, but the main structure was replaced with a fabricated steel backbone chassis and multi-tubular superstructure to support the polyester bodywork, complete with floor, to which the chassis was bolted. Seven colours were available and the finish was good, but the shape was a somewhat acquired taste. By using the 5's major components, the Département des Mines' requirements were not contravened.

Venturi 260 Cabriolet, 1991. MVS (Manufacture de Voitures de Sport) was founded in 1985 by Hervé Boulan to commercialize the original Ventury, a mid-engined fibre-glass coupé realized by Claude Poiraud and Gérard Godfroy, and presented at the 1984 Paris Salon. It finally used Renault's turbocharged, Douvrin-manufactured, 200bhp V6 for its 1986 Paris Salon commercial launch. In 1989, it was joined by a cabriolet and all versions, up to the 1998 Atlantique (300bhp), utilized the same basic power/transmission *bloc*. Venturi, as of 1990, also ran a 'Gentleman's Trophy' and was involved unsuccessfully in Formula One with Lamborghini. It was sold into the UK in rhd form 'in exclusive quantities'.

BIBLIOGRAPHY

(* denotes English translation of French title)

Bellu, R. *Toutes les Renault*, Delville, 1979 (2.85922.023.2)

Borgé, J. and Viasnoff, N. *La 4CV, la Première Voiture de l'Après-Guerre*, Balland, 1976 (2.7158.0080.0)

———. *Renault, l'Empire de Billancourt*, EPA, 1977 (2.85120.059.3)

Boulogne, J. *La Vie de Louis Renault*, Du Moulin d'Argent, 1931

Colin, M.-A. *La Renault Frégate de mon Père*, ETAI, 1997 (2.7268.8316.8)

Descombes, C. *Guide Alpine, tous les Modèles, Année par Année*, EPA, 1990 (2.85120.355.X)

———. *Berlinettes Alpine*, EPA, 1992 (2.85120.401.7)

Dumont, P. *Les Renault de Louis Renault*, Edifree, 1982

Dymock, E. *The Renault File, all Models since 1898*, Dove, 1998

Gérard, R. *Louis Renault, Seigneur d'Herqueville*, JCM, 1990 (2.902667.12.4)

Hatry, G. *Renault – Usine de Guerre 1914/1918*, Lafourcade, 1978

———. *Renault et la Compétition; l'Epoque Héroïque*, Lafourcade, 1979

———. *Louis Renault, Patron Absolu*, Lafourcade, 1981 (2.902667.07.8)

———. *Renault et la Compétition – les Folles Equipées*, JCM, 1985 (2.902667.10.8)

———. *Renault et l'Aviation*, JCM, 1988 (2.902667.11.6)

Hatry, G and Le Maître, C. *Dossiers Chronologiques Renault, V.1: 1899/1905*, Lafourcade, 1977

———. *Dossiers Chronologiques Renault, V.2: 1906/10* Lafourcade, 1978 (2.902667.02.7)

———. *Dossiers Chronologiques Renault, V.3: 1911/18*, Lafourcade, 1979 (2.902667.04.3)

———. *Dossiers Chronologiques Renault, V.4: 1919/23*, Lafourcade, 1980 (2.902667.05.1)

———. *Dossiers Chronologiques Renault, V.5: 1924/33*, Lafourcade, 1981 (2.902667.06.X)

———. *Dossiers Chronologiques Renault, V.6: 1934/44*, Lafourcade, 1982 (2.902667.08.6)

Latouille, J. and Felten, J.-M. *La 4CV, Historique, Evolution, Identification . . . etc.*, ETAI, 1977 (2.7268.8278.1)

Lesueur, P. *La 4CV de mon Père*, ETAI, 1996, (2.7268.8274.9)

Lesueur, P. and Pascal, D. *La Renault Dauphine de mon Père*, ETAI, 1997 (2.7268.8316.8)

Loubet, J.-L. *Renault – Cent Ans d'Histoire*, ETAI 1998 (2.7268.8332.X)

McLintock, J.D. *Renault, the Cars and the Charisma*, Stephens, 1983 (0.85059.582.7)

Meaney, P. *Renault 5 Turbo, the forgotten French Supercar*, Transport Source Books, 1996

Niéto, F. *A Century of Renault, in Pictures*,* Denoël, 1995 (2.207.24425)

Pagneux, D. *Album Dauphine*, EPA, 1994 (2.85120.429.7)

Pascal, D. *Alpine – Berlinettes . . . etc.*, EPA, 1982 (2.85120.148.4)

———. *Alpine Berlinette, L'Ecole de la Glisse*, ETAI, 1997 (2.7268.8326.5)

———. *L'Epopée de Renault*, Albin Michel, 1976 (2.226003.82.7)

Pouiboube, D. *Guide Renault, tous les Modèles, Année par Année*, EPA, 1992

Rhodes, A. *Louis Renault, a Biography*, Cassell, 1969

Richard, Y. *Renault 1898–1966*,* Foulis, 1965

Saint Loup. *Renault*,* Bodley Head, 1957

Seidler, E. *The Romance of Renault*, Edita, 1973

———. *The Renault Challenge*,* Edita, 1981 (2.8801.1173.5)

Sloniger, J. *Renault Guide*, Sports Car, 1960

Vermeylen, B. *La Renault 16 de mon Père*, ETAI, 1996 (2.7268.8276.5)

Voitures d'Autrefois – Automobiles Renault, ABC, 1974

INDEX